THE PHILOSOPHY OF David Hume

Eighteen of the most important books on Hume's philosophy reprinted in twenty volumes

Edited by
Lewis White Beck, The University of Rochester

A GARLAND SERIES

ESSAYS ON THE PRINCIPLES OF
Morality and Natural Religion

Henry Home, Lord Kames

Garland Publishing, Inc.
New York & London 1983

For a complete list of the titles in this series
see the final pages of this volume.

This facsimile has been made from a copy in the
Yale University Library.

Library of Congress Cataloging in Publication Data

Kames, Henry Home, Lord, 1696–1782.
Essays on the principles of morality and natural religion.

(The Philosophy of David Hume)
Reprint. Originally published: Edinburgh : R. Fleming,
1751.
1. Ethics.   I. Title.   II. Series.
BJ1005.K2   1983   170   83-9038
ISBN 0-8240-1781-1

Design by Jonathan Billing

The volumes in this series are printed on acid-free,
250-year-life paper.

Printed in the United States of America

ESSAYS

ON THE

PRINCIPLES

OF

MORALITY

AND

NATURAL RELIGION.

IN TWO PARTS.

EDINBURGH:

Printed by R. FLEMING, for A. KINCAID and
A. DONALDSON.
M.DCC.LI.

Advertisement.

IT is proper to acquaint the reader, before he enters on the following essays, that they are not thrown together without connection. The first, by the investigation of a particular fact, is designed to illustrate the nature of man, as a social being. The next considers him as the subject of morality. And as morality supposes freedom of action, this introduces the third essay, which is a disquisition on liberty and necessity. These make the first part of the work. The rest of the essays, ushered in by that on belief, hang upon each other. A plan is prosecuted, in support of the authority of our senses, external and internal; where it is occasionally shown, that our reasonings on some of the most important subjects, rest ultimately upon sense and feeling. This is illustrated, in a variety of instances; and from these, the author would gladly hope, that he has thrown new light upon the principles of human knowledge:----All to prepare the way, for a proof of the existence and perfections of the Deity, which is the chief aim in this undertaking.

dertaking. The author's manner of thinking, may, in some points, be esteemed bold and new. But freedom of thought, will not displease those who are led, in their inquiries, by the love of truth. To such only he writes: and with such, he will, at least, have the merit of a good aim; of having searched for truth, and endeavoured to promote the cause of virtue and natural religion.

ESSAY

ESSAYS

ON THE

PRINCIPLES of MORALITY

AND

NATURAL RELIGION.

PART I.

ESSAY I.

Of our ATTACHMENT *to* OBJECTS *of* DISTRESS.

A NOTED *French* author, who makes critical reflections upon poetry and painting, undertakes a subject, attempted by others unsuccessfully, which is, to account for the strong Attachment we have to Objects of Distress, not real objects only, but even fictitious. " It is not ea-
" sy (says he) to account for the pleasure
" we take in poetry and painting, which
" has often a strong resemblance to affliction,
" and of which the symptoms are sometimes
" the same with those of the most lively sor-
" row. The arts of poetry and painting are
" never more applauded than when they
" succeed in giving pain. A secret charm
" attaches us to representations of this na-
" ture, at the very time our heart, full of
" anguish, rises up against its proper pleasure.
" I dare

"I dare undertake this paradox, (continues "our author) and to explain the foundation "of this fort of pleasure which we have in po- "etry and painting; an undertaking that may "appear bold, if not rash, seeing it promises "to account to every man for what passes in "his own breast, and for the secret springs of "his approbation and dislike." Our author is extremely sensible of the difficulty of his subject; and no wonder, for it has a deep foundation in human nature.

Let us follow him in this difficult undertaking. He lays it down as a preliminary, that our wants and necessities are our only motives to action, and that in relieving us from them consists all natural pleasure: and in this, by the way, he agrees with Mr. *Locke* in his chapter of Power, *sect.* 37. and 43. This account of our natural pleasures shall be afterwards examined. What we have at present to attend to, is the following fundamental proposition laid down by our author: "That man by nature is designed an active "being:

"being: that inaction, whether of body or
"mind, draws on languor and difguft; and
"that this is a cogent motive to fly to any
"fort of occupation for relief. Thus (adds
"he) we fly by inftinct to every object that
"can excite our paffions, and keep us in agi-
"tation, not rebuted by the pain fuch objects
"often give us, which caufes vexatious days
"and fleeplefs nights: but man, notwith-
"ftanding, fuffers more by being without
"paffions, than by the agitation they occafi-
"on." This is the fum of his firft fection.
In the fecond he goes on to apply his principle to particular cafes. The firft he gives is
that of compaffion, whereby we are naturally impelled to dwell upon the miferies
and diftreffes of our fellow creatures, though
thereby we come to be partakers of their fuf-
ferings; an impulfe that he obferves is entirely owing to the above principle, which
makes us chufe occupation, however painful,
rather than be without action. Another is
that of publick executions. "We go in
"crouds (fays he) to a fpectacle the moft
"horrid

"horrid that man can behold, to see a poor
"wretch broke upon the wheel, burnt a-
"live, or his intrails torn out: the more
"dreadful the scene, the more numerous
"the spectators. Yet one might foresee,
"even without experience, that the cruel
"circumstances of the execution, the deep
"groans and anguish of a fellow creature,
"must make an impression, the pain of
"which is not to be effaced but by a long
"course of time. But the attraction of agi-
"tation is far more strong upon most people,
"than the joint powers of reflection and
"experience." He goes on to mention the strange delight the Roman people had in the entertainments of the amphitheatre; criminals exposed to be torn to pieces by wild beasts, and gladiators in troops set out to butcher one another. He takes this occasion to make the following observation upon the English nation: "So tender hearted is
"that people, that they observe humanity
"towards their greatest criminals. They al-
"low of no such thing as torture, alledging

"it

OBJECTS OF DISTRESS.

"it better to let a criminal go unpunished,
"than to expose an innocent person to those
"torments which are authorised in other
"Christian countries to extort a confession
"from the guilty. Yet this people, so respect-
"ful of their kind, have an infinite pleasure in
"prize-fighting, bull-beating, and such other
"savage spectacles." He concludes, with
showing, that it is this very horror of inaction, which makes people every day precipitate themselves into play, and deliver themselves over to cards and dice. " None but
" fools and sharpers (says he) are moved to
" play by hope of gain. The generality
" of mankind are directed by another mo-
" tive. They neglect those diversions where
" skill and address are required, chusing ra-
" ther to risque their fortunes at games of
" mere chance, which keep their minds in
" continual motion, and where every throw
" is decisive."

This is our author's account of the matter fairly stated. It has, I acknowledge, an
air of truth, but the following considerations

ons convince me that is not solid. In the first place, if the pain of inaction be the motive which carries us to such spectacles as are above mentioned, we must expect to find them frequented by none but those who are opprest with idleness. But this will not be found the truth of the matter. All sorts of people flock to such spectacles. Pictures of danger, or of distress, have a secret charm which attracts men from the most serious occupations, and operates equally upon the active and the indolent. In the next place, were there nothing in these spectacles to attract the mind, abstracting from the pain of inaction, there would be no such thing as a preference of one object to another, upon any other ground than that of agitation; and the more the mind was agitated, the greater would be the attraction of the object: but this is contrary to experience. There are many objects of horror and distaste, which agitate the mind exceedingly, that even the idlest fly from: and a more apt instance need not be given, than what our author

OBJECTS OF DISTRESS. 7

thor himself cites from Livy, † who, speaking of Antiochus Epiphanes, has the following words: *Gladiatorum munus Romanæ consuetudinis primò majore cum terrore hominum insuetorum ad tale spectaculum, quam voluptate dedit. Deinde sæpiùs dando, et familiare oculis gratumque id spectaculum fecit, et armorum studium plerisque juvenum accendit.* Such bloody spectacles behoved undoubtedly to make, at first, a greater impression than afterwards, when by repetition they were rendered familiar: yet this circumstance was so far from being an attraction to the Grecians, that it raised in them aversion and horror. Upon the same account, the Bear-garden, which is one of the chief entertainments of the English, is held in abhorrence by the French, and other polite nations. It is too savage an entertainment, to be relished by those of a refined taste.

If man is considered as a being, whose only view, in all his actions, is either to attain

† Lib. 41.

tain pleasure, or to avoid pain, we must conclude pleasure and pain to be his only impulses to action. Upon that supposition, it would be hard, if not impossible, to give any satisfactory account why we should chuse, with our eyes open, to frequent entertainments which must necessarily give us pain. But when we more attentively examine human nature, we discover many and various impulses to action, independent of pleasure and pain. Let us follow out this thought, because it may probably lead to a solution of the problem.

When we attend to the impressions made by external objects, or to any of our impressions, we find few of them so simple as to be altogether without modification. Impressions are either strong or weak, distinct or confused, &c. There is no division of impressions more comprehensive than into agreeable or disagreeable. Some slight impressions there may be, which give us little or no pleasure, or pain: but these may be
neglected

OBJECTS OF DISTRESS.

neglected in the present inquiry. The bulk of our impressions may certainly be distinguished into pleasant and painful. It is unnecessary, and would perhaps be in vain, to search for the cause of this difference among our impressions. More we cannot say than that such is the constitution of our nature, so contrived by the Author of all things, in order to answer wise and good purposes.

There is another circumstance to be attended to in these impressions; that *Desire* enters into some of them, *Aversion* into others. With regard to some objects, we feel a desire of possessing and enjoying them: other objects raise our aversion, and move us to avoid them. At the same time, desire and aversion are not separate impressions, but modifications only; each making a part of the total impression, raised by the agreeable, or disagreeable object. The pleasure, for example, of a fine garden, and the desire of possessing it, are not different impressions, but only parts of that entire impression which is caused by the object.

B

The impression made by any object is one, tho' it may be annalized into parts. It does not belong to the present subject, to inquire in what instances Desire is raised by agreeable objects; for desire does not accompany agreeable impressions in every instance: but it must be carefully attended to, that Aversion does not make a part, or enter into the composition of every painful impression. Objects of horror and terror, loathsome objects, and many others, raise aversion. But there are many impressions, some of them of the most painful sort, which have no degree of aversion in their composition. Grief is a most painful passion or impression, and yet is the farthest of any thing from being mixed with any degree of aversion. On the contrary, we cling to the object which raises our grief, and love to dwell upon it. Compassion is an instance of the like nature. Objects of distress raise no aversion in us, tho' they give us pain. Desire always makes a part of the impression, desire to afford relief.

In

In infancy, appetite and passion, and the desires and aversions accompanying them, are our sole impulses to action. But in the progress of life, when we learn to distinguish the objects around us as contributing to pleasure or pain, we acquire, by degrees, impulses to action of a different sort. Self-love is a strong motive to search about for every thing that may conduce to happiness. Self-love operates by means of reflection and experience; and every object, so soon as discovered to contribute to our happiness, raises of course a desire of possessing. Hence it is that pleasure and pain are the only motives to action, so far as self-love is concerned. But our appetites and affections, as above explained, are very different in their nature. These operate by direct impulse, without the intervention of reason, and answer to what is called instinct in brute creatures. As they are not influenced by any sort of reasoning, the view of shunning misery, or acquiring happiness, makes no part of the impulsive cause. It is true, that the

gra-

gratification of our affections and appetites is for the most part attended with pleasure; and it is also true, that, in giving way to a particular appetite, the view of pleasure may, by a reflex act, become an additional motive to the action. But these things must not be confounded with the direct impulse arising from the appetite or affection, which, as I have said, operates blindly, and in the way of instinct, without any view to consequences.

And to ascertain the distinction betwixt actions directed by self-love, and actions directed by particular appetites and passions, it must be further remarked, that though, for the most part, pleasure is the consequence of indulging appetites and passions, it is not necessarily, nor indeed universally so. If the latter be made out, the former will be evident; because there cannot be a necessary connection betwixt two things, which are in some instances separated. That pleasure is not always the consequence of indulging our appetites

petites and paffions, will be plain from induction. Revenge gratified againft the man we hate is attended with pleafure. 'Tis a very different cafe, where we have taken offence at a man we love. Friendfhip will not allow me, however offended, to hurt my friend. " I cannot find in my heart to do him mif- " chief; but I would have him made fenfible " of the wrong he has done me." Revenge, thus denied a vent, recoils and preys upon the vitals of the perfon offended. It difplays itfelf in peevifhnefs and bad humour, which muft work and ferment, till time, or acknowledgment of the wrong, carry it off. This fort of revenge is turned againft the man himfelf who is offended; and examples there are of perfons in this pettifh humour, working great mifchief to themfelves, in order to make the offenders fenfible of the wrong. Thus, nothing is more common than to find a young woman, difappointed in love, ready to throw herfelf away upon the firft worthlefs fellow that will ask her the queftion. This indeed is indulging the paffion of revenge,

venge, but without any concomitant pleaſure or ſatisfaction. Far from it: the greater the degree of indulgence, the greater the pain. My next inſtance will be ſtill more ſatisfactory. Every one muſt have obſerved, that when the paſſion of grief is at its height, the very nature of it is to ſhun and fly from every thing which tends to give eaſe or comfort. He ruſhes on to miſery, by a ſort of ſympathy with the perſon for whom he is grieved. Why ſhould I be happy when my friend is no more? is the language of this paſſion. In theſe circumſtances, the man is truly a ſelf-tormentor. And here we have a ſingular phœnomenon in human nature, an appetite after pain, an inclination to render one's ſelf miſerable. This goes further than even ſelf-murder; a crime that is never perpetrated but in order to put an end to miſery, when it riſes to ſuch an height as to be inſupportable.

We now ſee how imperfect the deſcription is of human nature, given by Mr. *Locke*,
and

OBJECTS OF DISTRESS.

and by our French author. They acknowledge no motive to action, but what arises from self-love; measures laid down to attain pleasure, or to shun pain. Our particular appetites and affections, and the desires and aversions involved in them, are left entirely out of the system. And yet we may say, with some degree of probability, that we are more influenced by these than by self-love. We further discover by this inquiry, what is of great importance to the subject in hand, that, as happiness is not always the impulsive motive to action, so neither is it always the effect of an indulged passion. Nay, we find this very singular phœnomenon in human nature a direct appetite or desire, in some instances, after pain. So various is human nature, and so complicated its acting powers, that it is not readily to be taken in at one view.

And now we return to our subject, after having unfolded those principles of action with which it is connected. It may be

gathered

gathered from what is above laid down, that nature, which designed us for society, has connected us strongly together, by a participation of the joys and miseries of our fellow creatures. We have a strong sympathy with them; we partake of their afflictions; we grieve with them and for them; and, in many instances, their misfortunes affect us equally with our own. Let it not therefore appear surprising, that people, instead of shunning objects of misery, chuse to dwell upon them; for this is truly as natural as indulging grief for our own misfortunes. And it must be observed at the same time, that this is wisely ordered by providence: were the social affections mixt with any degree of aversion, even when we suffer under them, we should be inclined, upon the first notice of an object of distress, to drive it from our sight and mind, instead of affording relief.

Nor ought we to judge of this principle, as any way vitious or faulty: for besides, that

OBJECTS OF DISTRESS.

that it is the great cement of human society, we ought to consider, that, as no state is exempt from misfortunes, mutual sympathy must greatly promote the security and happiness of mankind. And 'tis a much more comfortable situation, that the prosperity and preservation of each individual should be the care of the whole species, than that every man, as the single inhabitant of a desert island, should be left to stand or fall by himself, without prospect of regard, or assistance from others. Nor is this all. When we consider our own character and actions in a reflex view, we cannot help approving of this tenderness and sympathy in our nature; we are pleased with ourselves for being so constituted, we are conscious of inward merit; and this is a continual source of satisfaction.

To open this subject a little further, it must be observed, that naturally we have a strong desire to be acquainted with the history of our fellow creatures. We judge of their actions,

tions, approve or disapprove, condemn or acquit; and in this the busy mind has a wonderful delight. Nay, we go further. We enter deep into their concerns, take a side; we partake of joys and distresses, with those we favour, and show a proportional aversion to others. This turn of mind makes history, novels and plays the most universal and favourite entertainments. And indeed this is no more than what is to be expected from man as a sociable creature; and we may venture to affirm, that the most sociable have the greatest share of this sort of curiosity, and the strongest attachment to such entertainments.

Tragedy is an imitation or representation of human characters and actions. 'Tis a feigned history which generally makes a stronger impression, than what is real; because, if it be a work of genius, incidents will be chosen to make the deepest impressions, and will be so conducted, as to keep the mind in continual suspense and agitation,
beyond

OBJECTS OF DISTRESS.

beyond what commonly happens in real life. By a well wrought tragedy, all the social passions are roused. The first scene is scarce ended before we are engaged. We take a sudden affection to some of the personages represented. We come to be attached to them as to our bosom-friends, and hope and fear for them, as if the whole were a true history, instead of a fable.

To a dry philosopher, unacquainted with theatrical entertainments, it may appear surprising, that imitation should have such an effect upon the mind, and that the want of truth and reality should not prevent the operation of our passions. But whatever may be the physical cause, one thing is evident, that this aptitude of the mind of man, to receive impressions from feigned, as well as from real objects, contributes to the noblest purposes of life. Nothing conduces so much to improve the mind, and confirm it in virtue, as being continually employed in surveying the actions of others, entering into the concerns of the virtuous, approving of their conduct, condemning vice, and showing an abhorrence at it; for the mind acquires strength by exercise, as well as the body. But were there no opportunity for this sort of discipline, but from scenes of real life, the generality of men would be little the better for it, because such scenes do but rarely occur. They are not frequent even in history. But, in compositions where liberty is allowed of fiction, it must be want of genius, if the mind is not sufficiently exercised, till it acquire the greatest sensibility, and the most confirmed habits of virtue.

Thus, tragedy engages our affections, not less than true history. Friendship, concern for the virtuous, abhorrence of the vitious, compassion, hope, fear, and the whole train of the social passions, are roused and exercised by both of them equally.

This may appear to be a fair account of the attachment we have to theatrical entertertainments: but when the subject is more narrowly examined, some difficulties occur, to which the principles above laid down will scarce afford a satisfactory answer. 'Tis no wonder that young people flock to such entertainments. The love of novelty, desire of occupation, beauty of action, are strong attractions: and if one is once engaged, of whatever age, by entering into the interests of the personages represented, the attraction turns strong beyond measure, and the story must be followed out, whatever be the consequence. The foresight of running one's self into grief and affliction will not disengage. But people generally turn wise by experience; and it may appear surprising, when distress is the never failing effect of such entertainments, that persons of riper judgment should not shun them altogether. Does self-love ly asleep in this case, which is for ordinary so active a principle? When one considers the matter *a priori*, he will not hesitate to draw a conclusion to this purpose, that as repeated experience must, at the

long

long run, make us wife enough to keep out of harm's way; deep tragedies, for that reason, will be little frequented by perſons of reflexion. Yet the contrary is true in fact; the deepeſt tragedies being the moſt frequented by perſons of all ages, eſpecially by thoſe of delicate feelings, upon whom the ſtrongeſt impreſſions are made. A man of that character, who has ſcarce got the better of the deep diſtreſs he was thrown into the night before by a well acted tragedy, does, in his cloſet, coolly and deliberately reſolve to go to the next entertainment of the kind, without feeling the ſmalleſt obſtruction from ſelf-love.

This leads to a ſpeculation, perhaps one of the moſt curious that belongs to human nature. Contrary to what is generally underſtood, the above is a palpable proof, that even ſelf-love does not always operate to avoid pain and diſtreſs. In examining how this is brought about, there will be diſcovered an admirable contrivance in human nature,

ture, to give free scope to the social affections. Let us review what is above laid down: in the first place, that of the painful passions, some are accompanied with aversion, some with desire: in the next place, that of the painful passions, accompanied with desire, the gratification of some produces pleasure, such as hunger and thirst, revenge, &c. others pain and distress, such as grief. Now, upon the strictest examination, the following proposition will be found to hold true in fact; that the painful passions, which, in the direct feeling, are free from any degree of aversion, have as little of it in the reflex act. Or, to express the thing more familiarly, when we reflect upon the pain we have suffered by our concern for others, there is no degree of aversion mixt with the reflection, more than with the pain itself, which is the immediate effect of the object. For illustration's sake, let us compare the pain which arises from compassion with any bodily pain. Cutting one's flesh is not only accompanied with strong aversion in the di-

rect

rect feeling, but with an averfion equally ftrong in reflecting upon the action afterwards. We feel no fuch averfion in reflecting upon the mental pains above defcribed. On the contrary, when we reflect upon the pain which the misfortune of a friend gave us, the reflection is accompanied with an eminent degree of fatisfaction. We approve of ourfelves for fuffering with our friend, value ourfelves the more for that fuffering, and are ready to undergo chearfully the like diftrefs upon the like occafion.

When we examine thofe particular paffions, which though painful, not only in the firft impreffion, but alfo in the gratification, if I may call it fo, are yet accompanied with no averfion; we find they are all of the focial kind, arifing from that eminent principle of fympathy, which is the cement of human fociety. The focial paffions are accompanied with appetite for indulgence, when they give us pain, not lefs than when they give us pleafure. We fubmit willingly to to such painful passions, and reckon it no hardship to suffer under them. In this constitution, we have the consciousness of regularity and order, and that it is right and meet we should suffer after this manner. Thus the moral affections, even such of them as produce pain, both in the first feeling, and in the indulgence of the passion, are none of them attended with any degree of aversion, not even in reflecting upon the distress they often bring us under. And this observation tends to set the moral affections in a very distinguished point of view, in opposition to those that are either malevolent, or merely selfish.

Many and admirable are the springs of action in human nature, and not one more admirable than what is now unfolded. Compassion is a most valuable principle, which connects people in society by ties stronger than those of blood. Yet compassion is a painful emotion, and is often accompanied with pain in the indulgence. Were it accompanied with any degree of aversion,

verſion, even in reflecting upon the diſtreſs it occaſions, after the diſtreſs is over, that averſion would, by degrees, blunt the paſſion, and at length cure us of what we would be apt to reckon a weakneſs or diſeaſe. But the author of our nature has not left his work imperfect. He has given us this noble principle entire, without a counter-balance, ſo as to have a vigorous and univerſal operation. Far from having any averſion to pain, occaſioned by the ſocial principles, we reflect upon ſuch pain with ſatisfaction, and are willing to ſubmit to it upon all occaſions with chearfulneſs and heart-liking, juſt as much as if it were a real pleaſure.

AND now the cauſe of the attachment we have to Tragedy is fairly laid open, and comes out in the ſtrongeſt light. The ſocial paſſions, put in motion by it, are often the occaſion of diſtreſs to the ſpectators. But our nature is ſo happily conſtituted, that diſtreſs, occaſioned by the exerciſe of the ſocial paſſions, is not an object of the ſmalleſt

eft averfion to us, even when we reflect coolly and deliberately upon it. Self-love does not carry us to fhun affliction of this fort. On the contrary, we are fo framed, as willingly and chearfully to fubmit to it upon all occafions, as if it were a real and fubftantial good. And, thus, Tragedy is allowed to feize the mind with all the different charms which arife from the exercife of the focial paffions, without the leaft obftacle from felf-love.

HAD our author reflected on the fympathifing principle, by which we are led, as by a fecret charm, to partake of the miseries of others, he would have had no occafion of recurring to fo imperfect a principle as that of averfion to inaction, to explain this feeming paradox, that a man fhould voluntarily chufe to give himfelf pain. Without entering deep into philofophy, he might have had hints in abundance from common life to explain it. In every corner, perfons are to be met with of fuch a fympathifing temper,

per, as to chufe to fpend their lives with the difeafed and diftreffed. They partake with them in their afflictions, enter heartily into their concerns, and figh and groan with them. Thefe pafs their lives in fadnefs and defpondency, without having any other fatisfaction than what arifes upon the reflection of having done their duty.

AND if this account of the matter be juft, we may be affured, that thofe who are moft compaffionate in their temper will be fondeft of Tragedy, which affords them a large field for indulging the paffion. And indeed admirable are the effects brought about by this means: for, paffions as they gather ftrength by indulgence, fo they decay by want of exercife. Perfons in profperity, unacquainted with diftrefs and mifery, are apt to grow hard-hearted. Tragedy is an admirable refource in fuch a cafe. It ferves to humanize the temper, by fupplying feigned objects of pity, which have nearly the fame effect to exercife the paffion that

real

OBJECTS OF DISTRESS.

real objects have. And thus it is, that we are carried by a natural impulse to deal deep in affliction, occasioned by representations of feigned misfortunes; and the passion of pity alone would make us throng to such representations, were there nothing else to attract the mind, or to afford satisfaction.

It is owing to curiosity, that public executions are so much frequented. Sensible people endeavour to correct an appetite, which, upon indulgence, gives pain and aversion, and, upon reflection, is attended with no degree of self-approbation. Hence it is, that such spectacles are the entertainment of the vulgar chiefly, who allow themselves blindly to be led by the present instinct, with little attention whether it be conducive to their good or not.

And as for prize-fighting and gladiatorian shows, nothing animates and inspires us more than examples of courage and bravery. We catch the spirit of the actor, and turn

bold

bold and intrepid as he appears to be. On the other hand, we enter into the diſtreſſes of the vanquiſhed, and have a ſympathy for them in proportion to the gallantry of their behaviour. No wonder then, that ſuch ſhows are frequented by perſons of the beſt taſte. We are led by the ſame principle, that makes us fond of peruſing the lives of heroes and of conquerors. And it may be obſerved by-the-by, that ſuch ſpectacles have an admirable good effect in training up the youth to boldneſs and reſolution. In this, therefore, I ſee not that foreigners have reaſon to condemn the Engliſh taſte. Spectacles of this ſort deſerve encouragement from the ſtate, and to be made an object of public policy.

As for gaming, I cannot bring myſelf to think that there is any pleaſure in having the mind kept in ſuſpenſe, and as it were upon the rack, which muſt be the caſe of thoſe who venture their money at games of hazard. Inaction and idleneſs are not by

far

OBJECTS OF DISTRESS.

far so hard to bear. I am satisfied that the love of money is at the bottom. Nor is it a solid objection, that people will neglect games of skill and address, to venture their money at hazard; for this may be owing to indolence, diffidence, or impatience. There is indeed a curious speculation with regard to this article of gaming, that pleasure and pain attend good and bad success at play, independent of the money lost or win. It is a plain case, that good luck raises our spirits, as bad luck depresses them, without regard to consequences: and it seems extremely clear, that our concern at game, when we play for trifles, is owing to this very thing. What may be the root of this affection, is not so obvious. But as it is not necessarily connected with our present theme, I shall leave it to be investigated by others.

ESSAY II.

ESSAY II.

Of the FOUNDATION *and* PRINCIPLES *of the* LAW *of* NATURE.

INTRODUCTION.

SUPERFICIAL knowledge produces the boldest adventurers, because it gives no check to the imagination, when fired by a new thought. Writers of this stamp lay down plans, contrive models, and are hurried on to execution, by the pleasure of novelty, without considering whether, after all, there is any solid foundation to support the spacious edifice. It redounds not a little to the honour of some late inquirers after truth, that, subduing this bent of nature, they have submitted to the slow and more painful study of facts and experiments. Natural philosophy, in all its branches, is advanced by this laborious method. The accurate Mr. *Locke* has pursued the same track in the science of logicks, and has been followed by several ingenious writers. But

it seems to fare hard with the miftrefs-fcience, that lefs deference is paid to her than to her hand-maids. Every author exhibits a fyftem of morals, fuch as beft fuits his tafte and fancy. He frames regulations for human conduct, without confidering whether they arife out of human nature, or can be accommodated to it. And hence many airy fyftems that relate not more to man, than to many other beings. Authors of a warm imagination, and benevolent turn of mind, exalt man to the angelic nature, and compofe laws for his conduct, fo refin'd as to be far above the reach of humanity. Others of a contrary difpofition, forcing down all men to a level with the very loweft of their kind, affign them laws more fuitable to brutes than to rational beings. In abftract fcience, philofophers may more innocently indulge their fancies. The worft that can happen is, to miflead us in matters where error has little influence on practice: but they who deal in moral philofophy ought to be cautious, for their errors feldom fail to have a
bad

bad tendency. The exalting of nature above its standard is apt to disgust the mind, conscious of its weakness, and of its inability to attain such an uncommon degree of perfection. The debasing of nature tends to break the balance of the affections, by adding weight to the selfish and irregular appetites. A cruel effect this, but not the only bad one. The many clashing opinions about morality are apt to tempt readers, who have any hollowness of heart, to shake off all principles, and to give way to every appetite as it comes uppermost: and then adieu to a just tenor of life, and consistency of conduct.

These considerations give the author of this essay a just concern to proceed with the utmost circumspection in his inquiries, and to try his conclusions by their true touchstone, that of facts and experiments. Had this method been strictly followed, the world would not have been perplexed with many various and inconsistent systems, which unhappily

happily have rendered morality a difficult and intricate science. An attempt to restore it to its original simplicity and authority, must be approved of, however short one falls in the execution. Authors differ about the origin of the laws of nature, and they differ about the laws themselves. It will perhaps be found, that there is less difference about the former in reality, than in appearance. It were to be wished, that the different opinions about the latter could be as happily reconciled. But as the author acknowledges this to be above his reach, he must take up with a less agreeable task, which is to attempt a plan of the laws of nature, drawn from their proper source, without regarding authority.

CHAP.

CHAP. I.

Of the FOUNDATION *of the* LAW *of* NATURE.

IN searching for the foundation of the laws of our nature, the following reflections readily occur. In the first place, two things cannot be more intimately connected than a being and its actions; for the connection is that of cause and effect: such as the being is, such must its actions be. In the next place, the several classes into which nature has distributed living creatures, are not more distinguishable by an external form, than by an internal constitution, which manifests itself in a certain uniformity of conduct, peculiar to each species. In the third place, any action, conformable to the common nature of the species, is considered by us as regular and good: it is acting according to order, and according to nature. But if there exists a being, with a constitution different from that of its kind, the actions of this being, tho' agreeable to its own pe-

culiar

culiar conſtitution, will, to us, appear whimſical and diſorderly : we ſhall have a feeling of diſguſt, as if we ſaw a man with two heads or four hands. Theſe reflections lead us to the foundation of the laws of our nature. They are to be derived from the common nature of man, of which every perſon partakes who is not a monſter.

But as the above concluſion is the groundwork of all morality, it may not be improper to beſtow a few more words upon it. Looking around, we find creatures of very different kinds, both as to their external and internal conſtitutions. Each ſpecies having a peculiar nature, muſt have a peculiar rule of action reſulting from its nature. We find this to hold in fact; and it is extreme agreeable to obſerve how accurately the laws of each ſpecies, ariſing from its nature, are adjuſted to its external frame, and to the circumſtances in which it is placed, ſo as to procure the conveniencies of life in the beſt manner, and to produce regularity and conſiſtency

LAW OF NATURE.

fiftency of conduct. To give but one inftance. The laws, which govern fociable creatures, differ widely from thofe which govern the favage and folitary. Nothing more natural nor more orderly among folitary creatures, who have no mutual connection, than to make food one of another. But for creatures in fociety to live after this manner, behoved to be the effect of jarring and inconfiftent principles. No fuch diforderly appearance is to be met with upon the face of this globe. There is, as above obferved, a harmony betwixt the internal and external conftitution of the feveral claffes of animals; and this harmony obtains fo univerfally, as to afford a delightful profpect of deep defign regularly carried into execution. The common nature of every clafs of beings is felt by us as perfect; and, therefore, if, in any inftance, a particular being fwerve from the common nature of its kind, the action upon that account is accompanied with a fenfe of diforder and wrong. Thus, as we have a fenfe of right from every action,

tion, which is conformable to this common nature, the laws, which ought to govern every animal, are to be derived from no other fource than the common nature of the fpecies. In a word, it is according to order, that the different forts of living creatures fhould be governed by laws adapted to their peculiar nature. We confider it as fit and proper that it fhould be fo; and it is a beautiful fcene to find creatures acting according to their nature, and thereby acting uniformly, and according to a juft tenor of life.

THE force of this reafoning cannot, at any rate, be refifted by thofe who admit of final caufes. We make no difficulty to pronounce, that a fpecies of beings are made for fuch and fuch an end, who are of fuch and fuch a nature. A lion is made to purchafe the means of life by his claws. Why? becaufe fuch is his nature and conftitution. A man is made to purchafe the means of life by the help of others, in fociety. Why? be-

becaufe, from the conftitution both of his body and mind, he cannot live comfortably but in fociety. It is thus we difcover for what end we were defigned by nature, or the author of nature; and the fame chain of reafoning points out to us the laws by which we ought to regulate our actions. For, acting according to nature, is acting fo, as to anfwer the end of our creation.

CHAP. II.

Of the MORAL SENSE.

HAVING shown that the nature of man is the only foundation of the laws that ought to govern his actions, it will be necessary to trace out human nature with all the accuracy possible, so far as regards the present subject. If we can happily accomplish this undertaking, it will be easy, in the synthetical method, to deduce the laws which ought to regulate our conduct. And we shall examine, in the first place, after what manner we are related to beings and things about us; for this speculation will lead to the point in view.

As we are placed in a great world, surrounded with beings and things, some beneficial, others hurtful; we are so constituted, that scarce any of the objects of perception are indifferent to us. They either give us pleasure or pain. Sounds, tastes, and smells, are either agreeable or disagreeable. And the

the thing is most of all remarkable in the objects of sight, which affect us in a more lively manner than the objects of any other external sense. Thus, a spreading oak, a verdant plain, a large river, are objects which afford great delight. A rotten carcase, a distorted figure, create aversion, which, in some instances, goes the length of horror.

With regard to objects of sight, whatever gives pleasure, is said to be *Beautiful*; whatever gives pain, is said to be *Ugly*. The terms *Beauty* and *Uglines*, in their original signification, are confined to objects of sight: and indeed such objects, being more highly agreeable or disagreeable than others, deserve well to be distinguished by a proper name. But tho' this is the proper meaning of the terms Beauty and Uglinefs, yet, as it happens with words which convey a more lively idea than ordinary, the terms are applied in a figurative sense to almost every thing which carries a high relish or disgust, tho' not the object of sight, where
these

these feelings have not a proper name of their own. Thus, we talk of a beautiful theorem, a beautiful thought, and a beautiful action. And this way of speaking has, by common use, become so familiar, that it is scarce reckoned a figurative expression.

The pleasure and pain which arise from objects considered simply as existing, without relation to any end proposed, or any designing agent, are to be placed in the lowest rank or order of Beauty and Ugliness. But when external objects, such as works of art, are considered with relation to some end proposed, we feel a higher degree of pleasure or pain. Thus, a building regular in all its parts, pleases the eye, upon the very first view. But considered as a house for dwelling in, which is the end proposed, it pleases still more, supposing it to be well fitted to its end. A similar sensation arises in observing the operations of a well ordered state, where the parts are nicely adjusted to the ends of security and happiness.

This

LAW OF NATURE.

This perception of Beauty in works of art or design, which is produced not barely by a sight of the object, but by viewing the object in a certain light, as fitted to some use, and as related to some end, includes in it what is termed *Approbation*: for approbation, when applied to works of art, means, precisely, our being pleased with them, or conceiving them beautiful in the view of being fitted to their end. *Approbation* and *Disapprobation* do not apply to the first or lowest class of beautiful and ugly objects. To say that we approve of a sweet taste, or of a flowing river, is really saying no more, than barely that we are pleased with such objects. But the term is justly applied to works of art, because it means more than being pleased with such an object merely as existing. It imports a peculiar beauty, which is perceived upon considering the object as fitted to the use intended.

It must be further observed, to avoid obscurity, that the beauty, which arises from the relation

relation of an object to its end, is independent of the end itself, whether good or bad, whether beneficial or hurtful: for the feeling arises merely from considering its fitness to the end proposed, whatever that end be.

When we take the end itself under consideration, there is discovered a distinct modification of Beauty and Uglines, of a higher kind than the two former. A beneficial end proposed, strikes us with a very peculiar pleasure; and approbation belongs also to this feeling. Thus, the mechanism of a ship is beautiful, in the view of means well fitted to an end. But the end itself of carrying on commerce, and procuring so many conveniencies to mankind, exalts the object, and heightens our approbation and pleasure. By an End, I mean, that to which any thing is fitted, which it serves to procure and bring about, whether it be an ultimate end, or subordinate to something further. Hence, what is considered as an end in one view, may be considered as a means in another. But so far as it is confidered as an end, the degree of its Beauty depends upon the degree of its ufefulnefs. The feeling of Approbation here terminates upon the thing itfelf in many inftances, abftracted from the intention of an agent; which intention, coming into view as good or bad, gives rife to a modification of Beauty or Deformity, different from thofe above fet forth, as fhall be prefently explained. Let it be only kept in view, that, as the end or ufe of a thing is an object of greater dignity and importance than the means, the approbation beftowed on the former rifes higher than that beftowed on the latter.

These three orders of Beauty may be blended together in many different ways, to have very different effects. If an object, in itfelf beautiful, be ill fitted to its end, it will, upon the whole, be difagreeable. This may be exemplified, in a houfe regular in its architecture, and beautiful to the eye, but incommodious for dwelling. If there

is

is in an object an aptitude to a bad end, it will, upon the whole, be disagreeable, tho' it have the second modification of beauty in the greatest perfection. A constitution of government, formed with the most perfect art for enslaving the people, may be an instance of this. If the end proposed is good, but the object not well fitted to the end, it will be beautiful or ugly, as the goodness of the end, or unfitness of the means, are prevalent. Of this, instances will occur at first view, without being suggested.

The above modifications of beauty and deformity, apply to all objects animate and inanimate. A voluntary agent is an object which produces a peculiar modification of beauty and deformity, which may readily be distinguished in the feeling from all others. The actions of living creatures are more interesting than the actions of matter. The instincts, and principles of action of the former, give us more delight than the blind

powers

powers of the latter, or, in other words, are more beautiful. No one can doubt of this fact, who is in any degree conversant with the poets. In Homer every thing lives. Even darts and arrows are endued with voluntary motion. And we are sensible, that nothing animates a poem more than the frequent use of this figure.

And hence a new modification of the beauty and deformity of actions, considered as proceeding from intention, deliberation and choice. This modification, which is of the utmost importance in the science of morals, concerns principally human actions; for we discover little of intention, deliberation and choice in the actions of inferior creatures. Human actions are not only agreeable or disagreeable, beautiful or deformed, in the different views above mentioned, but are further distinguished in our feeling, as *fit*, *right* and *meet* to be done, or as *unfit*, *unmeet* and *wrong* to be done. These are simple feelings, capable of no definition, and

G which

which cannot otherways be explained, than by making use of the words that are appropriated to them. But let any man attentively examine what passes in his mind, when the object of his thought is an action proceeding from deliberate intention, and he will soon discover the meaning of these words, and the feelings which they denote. Let him but attend to a deliberate action suggested by filial piety, or one suggested by gratitude; such actions will not only be agreeable to him, and appear beautiful, but will be agreeable and beautiful as *fit*, *right* and *meet* to be done. He will approve of the action in that quality, and he will approve of the actor for having done his duty. This peculiar feeling, or modification of beauty and deformity in human actions, is known by the name of *moral beauty*, and *moral deformity*. In it consists the *morality* and *immorality* of human actions; and the power or faculty, by which we perceive this difference among actions, passes under the name of the *moral sense*.

It

LAW OF NATURE.

It is but a superficial account which is given of morality by most writers, that it depends upon Approbation and Disapprobation. For it is evident, that these terms are applicable to works of art, and to objects beneficial and hurtful, as well as to morality. It ought further to have been observed, that the approbation or disapprobation of actions, are feelings, very distinguishable from what relate to the objects now mentioned. Some actions are approved of as good and as fit, right and meet to be done; others are disapproved of as bad and unfit, unmeet and wrong to be done. In the one case, we approve of the actor as a good man; in the other, disapprove of him as a bad man. These feelings don't apply to objects as fitted to an end, nor even to the end itself, except as proceeding from deliberate intention. When a piece of work is well executed, we approve of the artificer for his skill, not for his goodness. Several things inanimate, as well as animate, serve to extreme good ends. We approve of these ends as useful in themselves, but not as morally

rally fit and right, where they are not considered as the result of intention.

Of all objects whatever, human actions are the most highly delightful or disgustful, and afford the greatest degree of beauty or deformity. In these every modification concurs: the fitness or unfitness of the means: the goodness or badness of the end: the intention of the actor, which gives them the peculiar character of *fit*, *right* and *meet*, or *unfit*, *wrong* and *unmeet*.

Thus we find the nature of man so constituted, as to approve of certain actions, and to disapprove of others; to consider some actions as *fit*, *right* and *meet* to be done, and to consider others as *unfit*, *unmeet* and *wrong*. What distinguishes actions, to make them objects of the one or other feeling, will be explained in the following chapter. And perhaps it will further appear, with regard to some of our actions, that the approbation, or disapprobation bestowed, has a more peculiar modification than has been hitherto observed, to be a foundation

tion for the well known terms of *duty* and *obligation*, and consequently for a rule of conduct, which, in the strictest sense, may be termed a law. But, at present, it is sufficient to have explained in general, that we are so constituted as to perceive or feel a Beauty and Deformity, and a Right and Wrong in actions. And this is what strongly characterises the laws which govern the actions of mankind. With regard to all other beings, we have no *Data* to discover the laws of their nature, other than their frame and constitution. We have the same *Data* to discover the laws of our own nature. And, we have, over and above, a peculiar feeling of approbation, or disapprobation, to point out to us what we ought to do, and what we ought not to do. And one thing is extremely remarkable, which will be explained afterwards, that the laws which are fitted to the nature of man, and to his external circumstances, are the same which we approve of by the moral sense.

C H A P.

CHAP. III.

Of Duty and Obligation.

THO' these terms are of the utmost importance in morals, I know not that any author has attempted to explain them, by pointing out those principles or feelings which they express. This defect I shall endeavour to supply, by tracing these terms to their proper source, without which the system of morals cannot be complete, because they point out to us the most precise and essential branch of morality.

Lord *Shaftesbury*, to whom the world is much indebted for his inestimable writings, has clearly and convincingly made out, " that virtue is the good, and vice the ill of " every one." But he has not proved virtue to be our duty, otherways than by showing it to be our interest, which does not come up to the idea of duty. For this term plainly implies somewhat indispensible in our conduct;

duct; what we ought to do, what we ought to submit to. Now a man may be considered as foolish, for acting against his interest, but he cannot be considered as wicked or vitious. His lordship, indeed, in his essay upon virtue *, points at an explanation of Duty and Obligation, by asserting the subordinacy of the self-affections to the social. But tho' he states this as a proposition to be made out, he drops it in the after part of his work, and never again brings it into view.

Mr. *Hutchison*, in his essay upon beauty and virtue †, founds the morality of actions on a certain quality of actions, which procures approbation and love to the agent. But this account of morality is imperfect, because it excludes justice, and every thing which may be strictly called Duty. The man who, confining himself to strict duty, is true to his word, and avoids harming others, is a just and moral man; is intitled to some

* Page 98. † Page 101.

some share of esteem, but will never be the object of love or friendship. He must show a disposition to the good of mankind, at least of his friends and neighbours: he must exert acts of humanity and benevolence, before he can hope to procure the affection of others.

But it is principally to be observed, that, in this account of morality, the terms *right*, *obligation*, *duty*, *ought* and *should*, have no distinct meaning; which shows that the entire foundation of morality is not taken in by this author. It is true, that, towards the close of his work, he endeavours to explain the meaning of the term *obligation*. But as criticising upon authors, those especially who have laid themselves out to advance the cause of virtue, is not the most agreeable task; I would not chuse to spend time, in showing that he is unsuccessful in his attempt. The slightest attention to the subject will make it evident. For his whole account of Obligation is no more than, " ei-
" ther

"ther a motive from self-interest, sufficient to "determine all those who duly consider it to "a certain course of action," which surely is not moral obligation; or "a determination, "without regard to our own interest, to "approve actions, and to perform them; "which determination shall also make us "displeased with ourselves, and uneasy upon "having acted contrary to it;" in which sense, he says, there is naturally an obligation upon all men to benevolence. But this account falls far short of the whole idea of obligation, and leaves no distinction betwixt it and a simple approbation or disapprobation of the moral sense; feelings that attend many actions, which by no means come under the notion of *obligation* or *duty*.

NEITHER is the author of the treatise upon human nature more successful, when he endeavours to resolve the moral sense into pure sympathy †. According to this author, there is no more in morality but approving

† Vol. 3. Part 3.

proving or disapproving of an action, after we discover by reflection that it tends to the good or hurt of society. This would be by far too faint a principle to controul our irregular appetites and passions. It would scarce be sufficient to restrain us from encroaching upon our friends and neighbours; and, with regard to strangers, would be the weakest of all restraints. We shall, by and by, show that morality has a more solid foundation. In the mean time, it is of importance to observe, that upon this author's system, as well as *Hutchison*'s, the noted terms of *duty, obligation, ought* and *should &c.* are perfectly unintelligible.

We shall now proceed to explain these terms, by pointing out the precise feelings which they express. And, in performing this task, there will be discovered a wonderful and beautiful contrivance of the Author of our nature, to give authority to morality, by putting the self-affections in a due subordination to the social. The moral sense has, in part,

part, been explained above; that, by it, we perceive some actions under the modification of being *fit*, *right*, and *meet* to be done, and others under the modification of being *unfit*, *unmeet* and *wrong*. When this observation is applied to particulars, it is an evident fact, that we have a sense of *fitness* in kindly and beneficent actions. We approve of ourselves and others for performing actions of this kind. As, on the other hand, we disapprove of the unsociable, peevish and hard-hearted. But, with regard to one set of actions, there is a further modification of the moral sense. Actions directed against others, by which they are hurt or prejudged in their persons, in their fame, or in their goods, are the objects of a peculiar feeling. They are perceived and felt not only as *unfit* to be done, but as absolutely *wrong* to be done, and what, at any rate, we *ought* not to do. What is here asserted, is a matter of fact, which can admit of no other proof than an appeal to every man's own feelings. Lay prejudice aside, and give fair play to the emotions of the heart. I ask no other concession. There is no man, however irregular in his life and manners, however poisoned by a wrong education, but must be sensible of this fact. And indeed the words which are to be found in all languages, and which are perfectly understood in the communication of sentiments, are an evident demonstration of it. *Duty, obligation, ought* and *should,* in their common meaning, would be empty sounds, unless upon supposition of such a feeling.

THE case is the same with regard to gratitude to benefactors, and performing of engagements. We feel these as our *duty* in the strictest sense, and as what we are indispensibly *obliged* to. We don't consider them as in any measure under our own power. We have the feeling of necessity, and of being bound and tied to performance, almost equally as if we were under some external compulsion.

IT is fit here to be remarked, that benevolent and generous actions are not the object

ject of this peculiar feeling. Hence, such actions, tho' considered as *fit* and *right* to be done, are not however considered to be our *duty*, but as virtuous actions beyond what is strictly our duty. Benevolence and generosity are more beautiful, and more attractive of love and esteem, than justice. Yet, not being so necessary to the support of society, they are left upon the general footing of approbatory pleasure; while justice, faith, truth, without which society could not at all subsist, are the objects of the above peculiar feeling, to take away all shadow of liberty, and to put us under a necessity of performance.

Doctor *Butler*, a manly and acute writer, has gone further than any other, to assign a just foundation for moral Duty. He considers * conscience or reflection, " as one
" principle of action, which, compared with
" the rest as they stand together in the na-
" ture of man, plainly bears upon it marks
" of

* Preface to the latter editions of his sermons.

" of authority over all the rest, and claims
" the absolute direction of them all, to al-
" low or forbid their gratification." And
his proof of this proposition is, " that a dif-
" approbation of reflection is in itself a prin-
" ciple manifestly superior to a mere pro-
" pension." Had this admirable author
handled the subject more professedly than
he had occasion to do in a preface, 'tis more
than likely he would have brought it out into its clearest light. But he has not said
enough to afford that light which the subject is capable of. For it may be observed, in the first place, that a disapprobation
of reflection is far from being the whole
of the matter. Such disapprobation is applied to morosenefs, selfishness, and many
other partial affections, which are, however,
not considered in a strict sense as contrary to
our duty. And it may be doubted, whether a disapprobation of reflection is, in every case, a principle superior to a mere propension. We disapprove of a man who neglects his private affairs, and gives himself

up

LAW OF NATURE.

up to love, hunting, or any other amusement: nay, he disapproves of himself. Yet from this we cannot fairly conclude, that he is guilty of any breach of duty, or that it is unlawful for him to follow his propension. We may observe, in the next place, what will be afterwards explained, that conscience, or the moral sense is none of our principles of action, but their guide and director. It is still of greater importance to observe, that the authority of conscience does not merely consist in an act of reflection. It proceeds from a direct feeling, which we have upon presenting the object, without the intervention of any sort of reflection. And the authority lyes in this circumstance, that we feel and perceive the action to be our duty, and what we are indispensibly bound to perform. It is in this manner, that the moral sense, with regard to some actions, plainly bears upon it the marks of authority over all our appetites and affections. It is the voice of God within us which commands our strictest obedience,

ence, just as much as when his will is declared by express revelation.

What is above laid down is an analysis of the moral sense, but not the whole of it. A very important branch still remains to be unfolded. And, indeed, the more we search into the works of nature, the more opportunity there is to admire the wisdom and goodness of the Sovereign Architect. In the matters above mentioned, performing of promises, gratitude, and abstaining from harming others, we have not only the peculiar feeling and sense of duty and obligation: in transgressing these duties we have not only the feeling of vice and wickedness, but we have further the sense of merited punishment, and dread of its being inflicted upon us. This dread may be but slight in the more venial transgressions. But, in crimes of a deep dye, it rises to a degree of anguish and despair. Hence that remorse of conscience, which histories are full of, upon the commission of certain crimes, and which proves the

the most severe of all tortures. This dread of merited punishment operates for the most part so strongly upon the imagination, that every unusual accident, every extraordinary misfortune is considered as a punishment purposely inflicted for the crime committed. While the guilty person is in prosperity, he makes a shift to blunt the stings of his conscience. But no sooner does he fall into distress, or into any depression of mind, than his conscience lays fast hold of him; his crime stares him in the face; and every accidental misfortune is converted into a real punishment. " And they said one " to another, we are verily guilty concern" ing our brother, in that we saw the anguish " of his soul when he besought us, and we " would not hear: therefore is this distress " come upon us. And *Reuben* answered " them, saying, Spake I not unto you, saying, " do not sin against the child? and you " would not hear. Therefore behold also " his blood is required †."

† Genesis, Chap. xlii. ver. 21, 22.

One material circumstance is here to be remarked, which makes a further difference betwixt the primary and secondary virtues. As justice, and the other primary virtues, are more essential to society than generosity, benevolence, or any other secondary virtue, they are likeways more universal. Friendship, generosity, softness of manners, form particular characters, and serve to distinguish one man from another. But the sense of justice, and of the other primary virtues, is universal. It belongs to man as such. Tho' it exists in very different degrees of strength, there perhaps never was a human creature absolutely void of it. And it makes a delightful appearance in the human constitution, that even where this sense is weak, as it is in some individuals, it notwithstanding retains its authority as the director of their conduct. If there is any sense of justice, or of abstaining from injury, it must distinguish Right from Wrong, what we *ought* to do from what we *ought not* to do; and, by that very distinguishing feeling, justly claims to be our guide

LAW OF NATURE.

guide and governor. This confideration may ferve to juftify human laws, which make no diftinction among men, as endued with a ftronger or weaker fenfe of morality.

AND here we muft paufe a moment, to indulge fome degree of admiration upon this part of the human fyftem. Man is evidently intended to live in fociety; and becaufe there can be no fociety among creatures who prey upon one another, it was neceffary, in the firft place, to provide againft mutual injuries. Further; man is the weakeft of all creatures feparately, and the very ftrongeft in fociety. Therefore mutual affiftance is the principal end of fociety. And to this end it was neceffary, that there fhould be mutual truft and reliance upon engagements, and that favours received fhould be thankfully repaid. Now nothing can be more finely adjufted than the human heart to anfwer thefe purpofes. 'Tis not fufficient, that we approve of every action which is effential to the prefervation of fociety. 'Tis not fufficient

ent, that we disapprove of every action which tends to its dissolution. A simple sense of approbation or disapprobation will scarce be sufficient to give these actions the sanction of a law. But the approbation in this case has the peculiar feeling of duty, that these actions are what we ought to perform, and what we are indispensibly bound to perform. This circumstance converts into a law what without it can only be considered as a rational measure, and a prudential rule of action. Nor is any thing omitted to give it the most complete character of a law. The transgression is attended with apprehension of punishment, nay with actual punishment; as every misfortune which befalls the transgressor is considered by him as a punishment. Nor is this the whole of the matter. Sympathy with our fellow-creatures is a principle implanted in the breast of every man: we cannot hurt another without suffering for it, which is an additional punishment. And we are still further punished for our injustice, or ingratitude, by incurring thereby the aversion and hatred of mankind.

CHAP.

CHAP. IV.

Of the DIFFERENT ORDERS *of* MORAL BEAUTY.

IT is a fact which will be univerfally admitted, that no man thinks fo highly of himfelf, or of another, for having done a juft, as for having done a generous action: yet every one muft be fenfible, that juftice is more effential than generofity to the order and prefervation of fociety ; and why we fhould place the greater merit upon the lefs effential action may appear unaccountable. This matter deferves to be examined, becaufe it gives a further opening to the fcience of morals.

UPON a fmall degree of reflection, it will appear, that the whole fyftem of morals is founded upon the fuppofition of liberty of action *. If actions were underftood to be

neceffary,

---

* Doctor Butler, preface to his fermons, page 11. fays, " Our conftitution is put into our own power: we are " charged with it ; and therefore are accountable for any " diforder or violation of it."

necessary, and no way under our power or controul, we could never conceive them as fit or unfit to be done; as what we are indispensibly bound to do or not to do. To have such a feeling of human actions, upon the supposition of necessity, would be as inconsistent as to have such a feeling of the actions of matter. The celebrated dispute about liberty and necessity is reserved to be discussed in a following essay. But without entering upon that subject at present, one fact is certain, that in acting we have a feeling of liberty and independency. We never do a wrong, however strong the motive be, which is not attended with a severe reflection, that we *might* have done otherways, and *ought* to have done otherways. Nay, during the very action, in the very time of it, we have a sense or feeling of wrong, and that we *ought* to forbear. So that the moral sense, both in the direct feeling, and in the act of reflection, plainly supposes and implies liberty of action.

THIS

This, if we mistake not, will clear the difficulty above stated. If in the moral sense be involved liberty of action, there must of consequence be the highest sense or feeling of morality where liberty is greatest. Now, in judging of human actions, those actions, which are essential to the order and preservation of society, are considered to be in a good measure necessary. It is our strict duty to be just and honest. We are bound by a law in our nature, which we ought not to transgress. No such feeling of duty or obligation attends those actions which come under the denomination of *generosity, greatness of mind, heroism.* Justice, therefore, is considered as less free than generosity; and, upon that very account, we ascribe less merit to the former, than to the latter. We ascribe no merit at all to an action which is altogether involuntary; and we ascribe more or less merit, in proportion as the action is more or less voluntary.

Thus there is discovered two ranks or classes of moral actions, which are different in their nature, and different as to the laws by which they are enforced. Those of the first rank, being essential to the subsistence of society, are entirely withdrawn from our election and choice. They are perceived as indispensibly obligatory upon us; and the transgression of the laws, which regulate this branch of our conduct, is attended with severe and never-failing punishment. In a word, there is not a characteristic of positive law which is not applicable, in the strictest sense, to these laws of nature; with this material difference, that the sanctions of these laws are greatly more efficacious than any have been that invented to enforce municipal laws. Those of the second rank, which contribute to the improvement of society, but are not strictly necessary to its subsistence, are left to our own choice. They have not the character of moral necessity impressed upon them, nor is the forbearance of them attended with the feeling of guilt. On the

the other hand, the actions which belong to this rank are the objects of the strongest feelings of moral beauty; of the highest degree of approbation, both from ourselves and others. Offices of undeserved kindness, requital of good for evil, generous toils and sufferings for the good of our country, come under this class. These are not made our *duty*. There is no motive to the performance, which, in any proper sense, can be called a law. But there are the strongest motives that can consist with perfect freedom. The performance is rewarded with a consciousness of self-merit, and with the praise and admiration of all the world, which are the highest and most refined pleasures that human nature is susceptible of.

There is so much of enthusiasm in this branch of moral beauty, that it is not wonderful to find persons of a free and generous turn of mind captivated with it, who are less attentive to the virtues of the

first

firſt claſs. The magnanimous, who cannot bear reſtraint, are more guided by generoſity than juſtice. Yet, as pain is a ſtronger motive to action than pleaſure, the remorſe which attends a breach of ſtrict duty is, with the bulk of mankind, a more powerful incitement to honeſty, than praiſe and ſelf-approbation are to generoſity. And there cannot be a more pregnant inſtance of wiſdom than this part of the human conſtitution; it being far more eſſential to ſociety, that all men be juſt and honeſt, than that they be patriots and heroes.

The ſum of what is above laid down is, that, with regard to actions of the firſt rank, the pain of tranſgreſſing the law is much greater than the pleaſure which reſults from obeying it. The contrary is the caſe of actions of the ſecond rank. The pleaſure ariſing from the performance is much greater than the pain of neglect. Among the vices oppoſite to the primary virtues, the
moſt

most striking appearances of moral deformity are found. Among the secondary virtues, the most striking appearances of moral beauty.

CHAP. V.

Of the PRINCIPLES *of* ACTION.

IN the three foregoing chapters we have taken some pains to inquire into the moral sense, and to annalise it into its different feelings. Our present task must be to inquire into those principles in our nature which move us to action. These are different subjects. For the moral sense, properly speaking, is not a principle which moves us to action. Its province is to instruct us, which of our principles of action we may indulge, and which of them we must restrain. It is the voice of God within us, informing us of our duty.

IN a treatise upon the law of nature it is of great importance to trace out the principles by which we are led to action. We have above observed, that the laws of nature can be no other than rules of action adapted to our nature. Now our nature, so far as
con-

concerns action, is made up of appetites, passions and affections, which are the principles of action, and of the moral sense, by which these principles are governed and directed. No action therefore is a duty, to the performance of which we are not prompted by some natural principle. To make such an action our duty, would be to lay down a rule of conduct contrary to our nature, or that has no foundation in our nature. Conscience, or the moral sense, may restrain us from actions to which we are incited by a natural principle: but conscience, or the moral sense, is not, in any case, the sole principle or motive of action. Nature has assigned it a different province. This is a truth which has been little attended to by those who have given us systems of natural laws. No wonder, therefore, they have wandered so far from truth. Let it be kept close in view, and it will put an end to many a controversy about these laws. For example, if it be laid down as a primary law of nature, that we are strictly bound to advance the

good

good of all, regarding our own intereſt no further than as it makes a part of the general happineſs, we may ſafely reject ſuch a law as inconſiſtent with our nature, unleſs it be made appear, that there is a principle of benevolence in man which prompts him to an equal purſuit of the happineſs of all. To found this diſintereſted ſcheme wholly upon the moral ſenſe, would be a fruitleſs endeavour. The moral ſenſe, as above obſerved, is our guide only, not our mover. Approbation or diſapprobation of theſe actions, to which, by ſome natural principle, we are antecedently directed, is all that can reſult from it. If it be laid down, on the other hand, that we ought only to regard ourſelves in all our actions, and that it is folly, if not vice, to concern ourſelves for others, ſuch a law can never be admitted, unleſs upon the ſuppoſition that ſelf-love is our only principle of action.

It is probable, that, in the following particular, man differs from the brute creation.

Brutes

Brutes are entirely governed by principles of action, which, in them, obtain the name of Instincts. They blindly follow their instincts, and are led by that instinct which is strongest for the time. It is *meet* and *fit* they should act after this manner, because it is acting according to the whole of their nature. But for man to allow himself to be led implicitly by instinct, or his principles of action, without check or controul, is not acting according to the whole of his nature. He is endued with a moral sense or conscience, to check and controul his principles of action, and to instruct him which of them he may indulge, and which of them he ought to restrain. This account of the brute creation is undoubtedly true in the main: whether so in every particular is of no importance to the present subject, being only suggested by way of contrast, to illustrate the peculiar nature of man.

A FULL account of our principles of action would be an endless theme. But as it is proposed

posed to confine the present short essay to the laws which govern social life, we shall have no occasion to inquire into any principles of action, but what are directed upon others; dropping these which have self alone for their object. And, in this inquiry, we set out with a most important question, *sciz.* In what sense we are to hold a principle of universal benevolence, as belonging to human nature? When we consider a single man, abstracted from all circumstances and all connections, we are not conscious of any benevolence to him: we feel nothing within us that prompts us to advance his happiness. If one is agreeable at first sight, and attracts any degree of affection, it is owing to looks, manner or behaviour. And for evidence of this, we are as apt to be disgusted at first sight, as to be pleased. Man is by nature a shy and timorous animal. Every new object gives an impression of fear, till, upon better acquaintance, it is discovered to be harmless. Thus an infant clings to its nurse upon the sight of a new face; and this

this natural dread is not removed but by long experience. If every human creature did produce affection in every other at first fight, children, by natural instinct, would be fond of strangers. But no such instinct discovers itself. Fondness is confined to the nurse, the parents, and those who are most about the child; 'till, by degrees, it opens to a sense of larger connections. This argument may be illustrated by a very low, but very apt instance. Dogs have, by nature, an affection for the human species; and, upon this account, puppies run to the first man they see, show marks of fondness, and play about his feet. There is no such general fondness of man to man by nature. Particular circumstances are always required to produce and call it forth. Distress indeed never fails to beget sympathy. The misery of the most unknown is a painful object, and we are prompted by nature to afford relief. But when there is nothing to call forth our sympathy; where there are no peculiar circumstances to inte-

L *rest*

rest us, or beget a connection, we rest in a state of indifference, and are not conscious of wishing either good or ill to the person. Those moralists, therefore, who require us to lay aside all partial affection, and to act upon a principle of general equal benevolence to all men, require us to act upon a principle which in truth has no place in our nature.

Notwithstanding of this it may be justly said, that man is endued with a principle of universal benevolence. For the happiness of mankind is an object agreeable to the mind in contemplation; and good men have a sensible pleasure in every study or pursuit by which they can promote it. It must indeed be acknowledged, that benevolence is not equally directed to all men, but gradually decreases, according to the distance of the object, 'till it dwindle away to nothing. But here comes in a happy contrivance of nature, to supply the want of benevolence towards distant objects; which is, to give power

er to an abstract term, such as our religion, our country, our government, or even mankind, to raise benevolence or publick spirit in the mind. The particular objects under each of these classes, considered singly and apart, may have little or no force to produce affection; but when comprehended under one general term, they become an object that dilates and warms the heart: and, in this way, man is enabled to embrace in his affection all mankind, and thereby prompted to publick spirited actions.

He must have a great share of indifference in his temper who can reflect upon this branch of human nature without some degree of emotion. There is perhaps not one scene to be met with in the natural or moral world, where more of design and of consummate wisdom are displayed, than in this under consideration. The authors, who, impressed with reverence for human nature, have endeavoured to exalt it to the highest pitch, could none of them stretch their imagination beyond a principle of equal and universal

niverſal benevolence. And a very fine ſcheme it is in idea. But unluckily it is entirely of the *Utopian* kind, altogether unfit for life and action. It has eſcaped the conſideration of theſe authors, that man is by nature of a limited capacity, and that his affection, by multiplication of objects, inſtead of being increaſed, is ſplit into parts, and weakened by diviſion. A principle of univerſal equal benevolence, by dividing the attention and affection, inſtead of promoting benevolent actions, would in reality be an obſtruction to them. The mind would be diſtracted by the multiplicity of objects that have an equal influence, ſo as to be eternally at a loſs where to ſet out. But the human ſyſtem is better adjuſted, than to admit of ſuch diſproportion betwixt ability and affection. The principal objects of man's love are his friends and relations. He has to ſpare for his neighbours. His affection leſſens gradually in proportion to the diſtance of the object, 'till it vaniſh altogether. But were this the whole of human nature, with regard to benevolence,

nevolence, man would be but an abject creature. By a very happy contrivance, objects which, because of their distance, have little or no influence, are made by accumulation, and by being gathered together, in one general view, to have the very strongest effect; exceeding in many instances the most lively affection that is bestowed upon particular objects. By this happy contrivance the attention of the mind, and its affections, are preserved entire, to be bestowed upon general objects, instead of being dissipated by an endless division. Nothing more ennobles human nature than this principle or spring of action; and, at the same time, nothing is more wonderful, than that a general term, to which a very faint, if any, idea is affixt, should be the foundation of a more intense affection than is bestowed, for the most part, upon particular objects, how attractive soever. When we talk of our country, our religion, our government, the ideas annexed to these general terms are at best obscure and indistinct. General terms are extremely useful

in

in language, serving, like mathematical signs, to communicate our thoughts in a summary way. But the use of them is not confined to language. They serve for a much nobler purpose, to excite us to generous and benevolent actions, of the most exalted kind; not confined to particulars, but grasping whole societies, towns, countries, kingdoms, nay, all mankind. By this curious mechanism, the defect of our nature is amply remedied. Distant objects, otherways insensible, are rendered conspicuous. Accumulation makes them great, and greatness brings them near the eye. The affection is preserved, to be bestowed entire, as upon a single object. And to say all in one word, this system of benevolence, which is really founded in human nature, and not the invention of man, is infinitely better contrived to advance the good and happiness of mankind, than any *Utopian* system that ever has been produced, by the warmest imagination.

UPON

Upon the opposite system of absolute selfishness, there is no occasion to lose a moment. It is evidently chimerical, because it has no foundation in human nature. It is not more certain, that there exists the creature man, than that he has principles of action directed entirely upon others; some to do them good, and others to do them mischief. Who can doubt of this, when friendship, compassion, gratitude on the one hand; and, on the other, malice and resentment are considered. It has indeed been observed, that we indulge such passions and affections merely for our own gratification. But no person can relish this observation, who is in any measure acquainted with human nature. The social affections are in fact the source of the deepest afflictions, as well as of the most exalted pleasures, as has been fully laid open in the foregoing essay. In a word, we are evidently formed by nature for society, and for indulging the social, as well as the selfish passions; and therefore, to contend, that we ought only to regard ourselves, and to be

influenced

influenced by no principles but what are selfish, is directly to fly in the face of nature, and to lay down a rule of conduct inconsistent with our nature.

These systems being laid aside, as widely erring from the nature of man, the way lyes open to come at what are his true and genuine principles of action. The first thing that nature consults, is the preservation of her creatures. Hence the love of life is made the strongest of all instincts. Upon the same foundation, pain is in a greater degree the object of aversion, than pleasure is of desire. Pain warns us of what tends to our dissolution, and so is a strong guard to self-preservation: Pleasure is often sought after unwarily, and by means dangerous to health and life. Pain comes in as a monitor of our danger; and nature, consulting our preservation in the first place, and our gratification only in the second, wisely gives pain more force to draw us back, than it gives pleasure to push us forward.

LAW OF NATURE.

THE second principle of action is self-love, or desire of our own happiness and good. This is a stronger principle than benevolence, or love bestowed upon others; and in that respect is wisely ordered, because every man has more power, knowledge, and opportunity to promote his own good, than that of others. Thus the good of individuals is principally trusted to their own care. It is agreeable to the limited nature of such a creature as man, that it should be so, and consequently it is wisely ordered that every man should have the strongest affection for himself.

THE above principles have *Self* for their object. The following regard others. Fidelity is undoubtedly a principle of action not of the weakest sort. Performance of promises, the standing true to engagements, and in general the executing of trusts, come under this head. Therefore friendship belongs to this principle, which supposes a mutual engagement; and also love to children, who by nature are entrusted to our care.

Gratitude is a fourth principle of action, universally acknowledged; and Benevolence possesses the last place, diversified by its objects, and exerting itself more vigorously, or more faintly, in proportion to the distance of particular objects, and the grandeur of those that are general. This principle of action has one remarkable modification, that it operates with much greater force to relieve those in distress, than to promote positive good. In the case of distress, sympathy comes to its aid, and, in that circumstance, it acquires the name of *compassion*.

These several principles of action are ordered, with admirable wisdom, to promote the general good in the best and most effectual manner. We act for the general good, when we act upon these principles, even when it is not our immediate aim. The general good is an object too sublime, and too remote, to be the sole impulsive motive to action. It is better ordered, that, in most instances, individuals should have a limited aim,
which

which they can readily accomplish. To every man is assigned his own task. And, if every man do his duty, the general good will be promoted much more successfully, than if it were the aim in every single action.

The above mentioned principles of action belong to man as such, and constitute what may be called the common nature of man. Many other principles exert themselves upon particular objects in the instinctive manner, without the intervention of any sort of reasoning or reflection, which also belong to man as such, appetite for food, lust, &c. Other particular appetites, passions and affections, such as ambition, avarice, envy, love of novelty, of grandeur, &c. constitute the peculiar nature of individuals; because these are diversified among individuals in very different degrees. It belongs to the science of Ethics, to treat of these particular principles of action. All that needs here be observed of them is, that it is the aim of the general principle of self-love to obtain gratification to these particular principles.

CHAP.

CHAP. VI.

Of the Source *of the* Laws *of* Nature, *according to some Authors.*

HAVING thus at full length explained the nature of man, so far as concerns the present subject, it may not be disagreeable to the reader, to have some relaxation, before he enters upon the remaining part of the work. We shall fill up this interval with a view of some opinions, about the foundation of the laws of nature, which we cannot help judging to be inaccurate, if not erroneous. The episode is, at the same time, strictly connected with the principal subject; because truth is always best illustrated by opposing it to error. That morality depends entirely on the will of God, and that his will creates the only obligation we ly under to be virtuous, is the opinion of several writers. This opinion, in one sense, is true; but far from being true in their sense who inculcate it. And, true or false, it does not

not advance us a single step in the knowledge of our duty. For what does it avail to know, that morality depends upon the will of God, 'till we once know what his will is? If it be said, there is an original revelation of it to us in our nature, this can only mean, that our nature itself makes us feel the distinction betwixt virtue and vice, which is the very doctrine above laid down. But, say they, God, from the purity and rectitude of his nature, cannot but approve of good actions, and disapprove of such as are otherways. Here they don't consider, that this argument supposes a distinction betwixt virtue and vice antecedent to the will of God. For if, abstracting from his will, virtue and vice were indifferent, which is supposed in the proposition, we have no *Data* from the purity of God's nature, or from any other principle, to conclude, that virtue is more the object of his choice than vice. But, further, the very supposition of the purity and rectitude of the nature of the Divine Being presupposes a taste, feeling, or knowledge in us of an essential difference betwixt virtue and vice. Therefore it can never be said, in any proper sense, that our only obligation to virtue is the will of God, seeing it is true, that, abstracting altogether from his will, there is an obligation to virtue founded in the very frame of our nature.

In one sense, indeed, it is true, that morality depends upon the will of God, who made us such as we are, with a moral sense to distinguish virtue from vice. But this is saying no more but that it is God's will, or that it is agreeable to him we should be virtuous. It is another thing to maintain, that man is indifferent to virtue and vice, and that he is under no obligation to the one more than to the other, unless so far as he is determined by the arbitrary will of a superior, or sovereign. That a being may be so framed as to answer this description, may be yielded. But, taking man as he is, endued with a moral sense, 'tis a direct contradiction to hold, that he is under no obligation to virtue,

virtue, other than the mere will of God. In this sense, morality no more depends upon the will of God, than upon our own will.

WE shall next take a view of a doctrine, which may be set in opposition to the foregoing, and that is Dr. *Clarke*'s demonstration of the unalterable obligation of moral duty. His proposition is, " That, from the
" eternal and necessary differences of things,
" there naturally and necessarily arise cer-
" tain moral obligations, which are of them-
" selves incumbent on all rational creatures,
" antecedent to all positive institution, and
" to all expectation of reward or punish-
" ment." And this proposition he demonstrates in the following manner: " That
" there is a fitness of certain circumstances
" to certain persons, and an unfitness of o-
" thers, antecedent to positive laws; and that,
" from the different relations of different
" things, there arises a fitness and unfitness
" of certain behaviour of some persons. For
" instance, God is superior to man, and
" there-

" therefore it is fit that man should worship
" him."

If this demonstration, as it is called, be the only or principal foundation of morals, unlucky it is, that a doctrine of such importance should have so long been hid from the publick. The antients, however, carried the obligation of morals perhaps as far as this eminent divine does. And now that the important discovery is made, it is not likely to do great service; considering how little the bulk of mankind are able to enter into abstruse reasoning, and how little influence such reasoning generally has after it is apprehended.

But abstruseness is not the only imperfection of this celebrated argument. It appears to me altogether inconclusive. Laying aside perception and feeling, upon which the doctor founds no part of his demonstration, I should be utterly at a loss, from any given relation betwixt persons, to draw a conclusion

sion of the fitness or unfitness of a certain course of behaviour. " God is our su-" perior, and therefore it is fit we should " worship him." But here I put the question, upon what principle of reason does this conclusion rest? where is the connecting proposition by means of which the inference is drawn? Here the doctor must be utterly at a loss. For the truth of the matter is, that the terms *fitness* and *unfitness*, in their present signification, depend entirely upon the moral sense. *Fitness* and *unfitness*, with regard to a certain end or purpose, are qualities of actions which may be gathered from experience. But *fitness* or *unfitness* of actions, as importing *right* or *wrong*, as denoting what we *ought* to do, or abstain from, have truly no meaning, unless upon supposition of a moral sense, which this learned divine never once dreams of taking into his argument. The doctor's error therefore is a common one, that he endeavours to substitute reason in place of feeling. The fitness of worshipping our Creator was obvious

ous to him, as it is to every man, because it is founded in our very nature. It is equally obvious with the preference of honesty to dishonesty. His only mistake is, that, overlooking the *law written in his own heart*, he vainly imagines that his metaphysical argument is just, because the consequence he draws from it happens to be true. And to satisfy even his most devoted disciples, that this is the case, let us only suppose, that man, by nature, had no approbatory or disapprobatory feeling of actions, it could never be evinced, by any abstract argument whatever, that the worship of the Deity is his duty, or, in the moral sense of fitness, that it is more fit for him to be honest than to be dishonest.

AND, upon this head, we will take the liberty to add, because it is of importance to the subject in general, that, supposing our duty could be made plain to us, by an abstract chain of reasoning, yet we have good ground to conclude, from analogy, that the Author of nature has not left our actions to
be

be directed by so weak a principle as reason: and a weak principle it must be to the bulk of mankind, who have little capacity to enter into abstract reasoning; whatever effect it may have upon the learned and contemplative. Nature has dealt more kindly by us. We are compelled by strong and evident feelings, to perform all the different duties of life. Self-preservation is not left to the conduct of reason, but is guarded by the strongest instinct, which makes us carefully, or rather mechanically, avoid every appearance of danger. The propagation of the species is enforced by the most importunate of all appetites, and the care of our offspring by a lively and constant affection. Is nature so deficient, as to leave the duty we owe our neighbour, which stands in the first rank of duties, to be directed by cool reasoning? This is not according to the analogy of nature, nor is it fact: witness compassion, friendship, benevolence, and all the tribe of the social affections. Neither is common justice left upon this footing, the

most

most useful, tho' not the most exalted virtue. The transgression of it is attended with a severe feeling of disapprobation, and also enforced by other feelings still more cogent and authoritative.

A LATE author *, whom I shall just mention by the way, gives a whimsical system of morals. He endeavours to reduce all crimes to that of telling a lie; and, because telling a lie is immoral, he concludes, that the several crimes he mentions are immoral. Robbery, for example, is acting or telling a lie; because it is in effect saying, that the goods I seise are mine. Adultery is acting or telling a lie, because it is in effect maintaining that my neighbour's wife is not his, but mine. But not to insist upon the folly of giving all crimes the same character, and confounding their nature, it appears evident, that, in this argument, the very thing is taken for granted which is to be proved. For why is it a virtual lie to rob one of his goods? Is

* Woolaston.

it not by imposing upon mankind, who must presume those goods to be mine, which I take as my own? But does not this evidently presuppose a difference betwixt *meum* and *tuum*, and that I ought not to make free with another's property without his consent? For what other reason are the goods presumed to be mine, but that it is unlawful to meddle with what belongs to another? The same observation will apply to all his other transmutations; for, in acting or telling the lie, it is constantly taken for granted, that the action is wrong in itself. And this very wrong is the circumstance which is supposed, in the reasoning, to impose upon the spectators. The error therefore of this author is of the same nature with Dr. *Clark*'s, in his system above examined. It is an evident *petitio principii*: the very thing is taken for granted which is undertaken to be proved. With regard to the present subject, we have no occasion further to observe of this curious author, that when he draws so strong consequences from telling a lie, it was to be expected he should have

have set in the clearest light the immorality of that action. But this he does not so much as attempt, leaving it upon the conviction of one's own mind. This indeed he might safely do; but not more safely than to leave upon the same conviction all the other crimes he treats of.

CHAP. VII.

Of JUSTICE and INJUSTICE.

JUSTICE is that moral virtue which guards property, and gives authority to covenants. And as it is made out above, that justice, being essentially necessary to the maintenance of society, is one of those primary virtues which are enforced by the strongest natural laws, it would be unnecessary to say more upon the subject, were it not for a doctrine espoused by the author of a treatise upon human nature, that justice, so far from being one of the primary virtues, is not even a natural virtue, but established in society by a sort of tacit convention, founded upon a notion of public interest. The figure which this author deservedly makes in the learned world, is too considerable, to admit of his being past over in silence. And as it is of great importance to creatures who live in society, to have justice established upon its most solid foundation, a chapter expresly upon
this

this subject may perhaps not be unacceptable to the reader.

Our author's doctrine, so far as it concerns that branch of justice by which property is secured, comes to this; that, in a state of nature, there can be no such thing as property; and that the idea of property arises, after justice is established by convention, whereby every one is secured in his possessions. In opposition to this singular doctrine, there is no difficulty to make out, that we have an idea of property, antecedent to any sort of agreement or convention; that property is founded on a natural principle; and that violation of property is attended with remorse, and a sense of breach of duty. In following out this subject, it will appear how admirably the springs of human nature are adapted one to another, and to external circumstances.

Man is by nature fitted for labour, and his enjoyment lyes in action. To this internal

nal constitution his external circumstances are finely adapted. The surface of this globe does scarce yield spontaneously food for the greatest savages; but, by labour and industry, it is made to furnish not only the conveniencies, but even the luxuries of life. In this situation, it is wisely ordered, that man should labour for himself and his family, by providing a stock of necessaries for them, before he think of serving others. The great principle of self-preservation directs him to this course. Now this very disposition of providing against want, which is common to man with many other creatures, involves the idea of property. The ground I cultivate, and the house I build, must be considered as mine, otherways I labour to no purpose. There is a peculiar connection betwixt a man and the fruits of his industry felt by every one; which is the very thing we call property. Were all the conveniencies of life, like air and water, provided to our hand without labour, or were we disposed to labour for the publick, without any selfish affections, there would be no sense of property, at least such a sense would be superfluous and unnecessary. But when self-preservation, the most eminent of our principles of action, directs every individual to labour for himself in the first place; man, without a sense or feeling of property, would be an absurd being. Every man therefore must have a notion of property, with regard to the things acquired by his own labour, for this is the very meaning of working for one's self: property, so far, is necessarily connected with self-preservation. But the idea of property is essentially the same, whether it relate to myself, or to another. There is no difference, but what is felt in surveying the goods of any two indifferent persons. And, were it consistent for a man to have the idea of his own property, without having a notion of property in another; such a man would be a very imperfect being, and altogether unqualified for society. If it could be made out, that such is the constitution of mankind in general, I should be much disposed

posed to believe that we were made by a fortuitous concourse of atoms. But the constitution of man is more wisely framed, and more happily adjusted to his external circumstances. Not only man, but all provident creatures who have the hording quality, are endued with the sense or feeling of property; which effectually secures each individual, in the enjoyment of the fruits of its own labour. And accordingly we find, in perusing the history of mankind, as far back as we have any traces of it, that there never has been, among any people or tribe, such a thing as the possession of goods in common. For, even before agriculture was invented, when men lived upon the natural fruits of the earth, tho' the plenty of pasture made separate possessions unnecessary, yet individuals had their own cattle, and enjoyed the produce of their cattle separately.

And it must not be overlooked, that this sense of property is fortified by another principle. Every man has a peculiar affection

for

for what he possesses, exclusive of others, and for what he calls his *own*. He applies his skill and industry with great alacrity to improve his own subject: his affection to it grows with the time of his possession; and he puts a much greater value upon it, than upon any subject of the same kind that belongs to another.

Here then is property established by the constitution of our nature, antecedent to all human conventions. We are led by nature to consider goods acquired by our industry and labour as belonging to us, and as our own. We have the sense or feeling of property, and conceive these goods to be our own, just as much as we conceive our hands, our feet, and our other members to be our own; and we have a sense or feeling equally clear of the property of others. What is here asserted is a matter of fact, of which there can be no other decisive evidence, than to appeal to every man's own feelings. At the same time we need scarce any other proof of this

fact

fact, than that *yours* and *mine* are terms familiar with the greatest savages, and even with children. They must have feelings which correspond to these terms; otherways the terms would not be intelligible to them.

But this is not all that is involved in the sense or feeling of property. We not only suffer pain in having our goods taken from us by force; for that would happen were they destroyed or lost by accident. We have the feeling of *wrong* and *injustice*. The person who robs us has the same feeling, and every mortal who beholds the action considers it as vicious and contrary to *right*.

But it is not sufficient to have overturned the foundation of our author's doctrine. We will proceed to make some observations upon it, to show how ill it hangs together.

And, in the first place, he appears to reason not altogether consistently in making out his system. He founds justice on a general
sense

sense of common interest *. And yet, at no greater distance than a few pages, he endeavours to make out †, and does it successfully, that public interest is a motive too remote and too sublime to affect the generality of mankind, and to operate, with any force, in actions so contrary to private interest as are frequently those of justice, and common honesty.

In the second place, abstracting from the sense of property, it does not appear, that a sense of common interest would necessarily lead to such a regulation, as that every man should have the undisturbed enjoyment of what he has acquired by his industry or good fortune. Supposing no sense of property, I do not see it inconsistent with society, to have a Lacedemonian constitution, that every man may lawfully take what by address he can make himself master of, without force or violence. The depriving us of that to which we have no affection, would

be

* Vol. 3. p. 59. † Vol. 3. p. 43.

be doing little more than drinking in our brook, or breathing in our air. At any rate, such a refined regulation would never be considered of importance enough, to be established, upon the very commencement of society. It must come late, if at all, and be the effect of long experience, and great refinement in the art of living. It is very true, that, abstaining from the goods of others is a regulation, without which society cannot well subsist. But the necessity of this regulation arises from the sense of property, without which a man would suffer little pain in losing his goods, and would have no feeling of wrong or injustice. There does not appear any way to evade the force of the above reasoning, other than peremptorily to deny the reality of the sense of property. Others may, but our author, I think, cannot with a good grace do it. An appeal may be safely made to his own authority. For is it not evidently this sense, which has suggested to him the necessity, in the institution of every society, to secure individuals in their

pos-

possessions? He cannot but be sensible, that, abstracting from the affection for property, the necessity would be just nothing at all. But our feelings operate silently and imperceptibly; and there is nothing more common than to strain for far-fetched arguments in support of conclusions which are suggested by the simplest and most obvious feelings.

A THIRD observation is, that since our author resolves all virtue into sympathy, why should he with-hold the same principle from being the foundation of justice? why should not sympathy give us a painful sensation, in depriving our neighbour of the goods he has acquired by industry, as well as in depriving him of his life or limb? For it is a fact too evident to be denied, that many men are more uneasy at the loss of their goods, than at the loss of a member.

AND, in the last place, were justice only founded on a general sense of common interest

tereſt, it behoved to be the weakeſt feeling in human nature, eſpecially where injuſtice committed againſt a ſtranger is, with whom we are not connected by any degree of benevolence. Now this is contrary to all experience. The ſenſe of injuſtice is one of the ſtrongeſt that belongs to humanity, and is attended with many peculiar modifications, *viz.* a feeling of acting contrary to the ſtricteſt obligations of duty, and a feeling of merited puniſhment for the wrong committed. Had our author but once reflected upon theſe peculiar feelings, he never could have been ſatisfied with the ſlight foundation he gives to juſtice; for theſe feelings are altogether unaccountable upon his ſyſtem.

THAT branch of juſtice, which regards promiſes and covenants, appears alſo to have a moſt ſolid foundation in human nature; notwithſtanding of what is laid down by our author in two diſtinct propoſitions †, " That " a promiſe would not be intelligible, before

" human

† Page 102.

"human conventions had established it;
"and that even, if it were intelligible, it
"would not be attended with any moral
"obligation." As man is framed for society, mutual trust and confidence, without which there can be no society, enter into the character of the human species. Correspondent to these, are the principles of veracity and fidelity. And, in this particular, among many, it is admirable to observe how accurately these principles are adapted to each other. Veracity and fidelity would be of no significancy, were men not disposed to have faith, and to rely upon what is said to them, whether in the way of evidence or engagement. Faith and trust, on the other hand, would be very hurtful principles, were mankind void of veracity and fidelity: for, upon that supposition, the world would be over-run with fraud and deceit. Supposing a society once established, the security of property, as well as of life, is indeed essentially necessary to its continuance and preservation. For, were

men

men in danger from their fellows, the condition of man behoved to be the same with that of savage animals, who, upon that very account, shun all manner of commerce. But fidelity and veracity are still more essential to society, because, without these principles, there cannot be such a thing as society at all: it could never have a beginning. 'Tis justly observed by our author, that man, in a solitary state, is the most helpless of beings; and that by society alone he is enabled to supply his defects, and to acquire a superiority over his fellow creatures; that by conjunction of forces, our power is augmented; by partition of employments, we work to better purpose; and, by mutual succour, we acquire security. But, without mutual fidelity and trust, we could enjoy none of these advantages: without them, we could not have any comfortable intercourse with one another: so that they are necessary even to the constitution of society. Hence it is, that treachery is the vilest of crimes, and what mankind have ever held in the

utmost

utmoſt abhorrence. It is worſe than murder, becauſe it forms a character, and is directed againſt all mankind; whereas, murder is only a tranſitory act, directed againſt a ſingle perſon. Infidelity is of the ſame ſpecies with treachery. The eſſence of both crimes is the ſame, to wit, breach of truſt. Treachery has only this aggravating circumſtance, that it turns the confidence repoſed in me, againſt the friend who truſts me. Now breach of promiſe is a ſpecies of infidelity; and therefore our author has but a ſingle choice. He muſt either maintain, that treachery is no crime, or that breach of promiſe is a crime. And, in fact, that it is ſo, every man muſt bear evidence to himſelf. The performance of a deliberate promiſe has, in all ages, been conſidered as a duty. We have that ſenſe and feeling of a promiſe, as what we are bound to perform by a ſtrict obligation; and the breach of promiſe is attended with the ſame natural ſtings, which attend other crimes, *ſciz.* remorſe, and merited puniſhment.

It is evident from the above, that it is but an imperfect conception of a promise to consider it as our author does *, with relation only to the person who makes the promise. In this internal act two persons are concerned; the person who makes the promise, and the person to whom the promise is made. Were there by nature no trust nor reliance upon promises, breach of promise would be a matter of indifferency. Therefore the essence of a promise consists in keeping faith. The reliance upon us, produced by our own act, constitutes the obligation. We feel ourselves bound to perform: we consider it as our duty. And when we violate our engagement, we have a sense of moral turpitude in disappointing the person who relied upon our faith.

We shall close this subject, concerning the foundation of justice, with a general reflection. Running over every branch of our duty, what concerns ourselves as well as our neigh-

* Vol. 3. p. 122.

neighbours, we find, that nature has been more provident, than to trust us entirely to the guidance of cool reason. It is observed above, that our duty is enforced by instinct and appetite, as well as it is directed by reason. Now, if man be a social being, and justice essential to society, it is not according to the analogy of nature, that we should be left to investigate this branch of our duty by a chain of reasoning, especially where the reasoning turns upon so remote an object as that of publick good. May we not apply to justice, what is so beautifully reasoned concerning society, in a dialogue upon happiness *: "If society be thus agreeable " to our nature, is there nothing within us " to excite and lead us to it? no impulse; " no preparation of faculties? It would be " strange if there should not." If we are fitted by our nature for society; if pity, benevolence, friendship, love, the general dislike of solitude, and desire of company, are natural affections, all of them conducive to
society,

* P. 155.

society, it would be strange if there should be no natural affections, no preparation of faculties, to direct us to do justice, which is so essential to society. But nature has not failed us here, more than in the other parts of our constitution. We have a feeling of property; we have a feeling of obligation to perform our engagements; and we have a feeling of wrong in encroaching upon property, and in being untrue to our engagements. Society could not subsist without these affections, more than it could subsist without the social affections properly so called. We have reason, *a priori*, to conclude equally in favours of both, and we find, upon examination, our conclusion to be just.

CHAP. VIII.

Of the PRIMARY LAWS *of* NATURE.

WE are now come to the thing principally intended in this essay, which is to give a general view of the primary laws of nature. Action ought to be the end and aim of all our inquiries; without which, moral, as well as metaphysical, reasonings are but empty speculation. And, as life and manners are more peculiarly the object of the moral science, it was to be expected, that the weight and importance of the subject, should have brought authors to one way of thinking. But it is lamentable to find the world divided about these primary laws, almost as much as they commonly are about the most airy and abstract points. Some authors acknowledge no principle in man, but what is altogether selfish; and it is curious to observe how they wrest and torture every social principle, to give it the appearance of selfishness. Others exalt human nature much above

bove its just standard, give no quarter to selfishness, but consider man as bound to direct every action to the good of the whole, and not to prefer his own interest to that of others. The celebrated lord *Shaftesbury* goes so far as not to admit of any thing like partial benevolence; holding, that if it is not entire, and directed to the whole species, it is not benevolence at all. It is not difficult to assign a cause for such difference in opinion; tho' it may appear strange, that authors should differ so widely upon a subject, which every man ought to be acquainted with, because the subject is his own constitution. There is nothing more common in philosophy, as well as in life and action, than to build castles in the air. Impatient of the slow and cold method of induction, we fly to systems, which every writer takes the liberty of framing, according to his own taste and fancy. Fond of the fabric which he himself has erected, 'tis far from his thoughts to subject it to examination, by trying whether it will stand the test of stubborn facts. Men of narrow minds and contracted principles, naturally fall in with the selfish system. The system of universal benevolence attracts the generous and warm-hearted. In the midst of various and opposite opinions, the purpose of this essay is to search for truth by the patient method of induction; and, after what is above laid down, it will not be difficult to find it.

Let us only recapitulate, that the principles of action furnish motives to action, and that the moral sense is given as an instructor to regulate our actions, to enforce one motive, to restrain another, and to prefer one to another, when they are in competition. Hence the laws of nature may be defined to be *rules of our conduct and behaviour, founded on natural principles, approved of by the moral sense, and enforced by natural rewards and punishments.*

In

In searching for these laws, it must be obvious, that we *may* safely indulge every principle of action, where the action is not disapproved of by the moral sense, and that we *ought* to perform every action which the moral sense informs us to be our duty. From this short proposition, may be readily deduced all the laws of nature which govern human actions. Tho', in the present essay, the duty which a man owes to himself, where others are not concerned, is not comprehended.

And, with regard to our general principles of action, self-preservation being the leading principle, it is hard to say, that any means, strictly speaking, are unlawful, to attain that end. If two men in a ship-wreck get hold at the same instant of a plank, which is not bulky enough to support both, it is lawful for the one to thrust off the other, in order to save his own life. This action is not condemned by the moral sense: It is not attended with any feeling of wrong. In like manner

manner, it is lawful for a man to seize upon food wherever he can find it, to keep himself from dying of hunger.

Upon the same principle, it is lawful for a man to save a member of his own body, at the expence of another's member, if both cannot be saved. A man will scarce have any consciousness of wrong in so doing. But it will hardly be allowed in morality, to save a member at the expence of another's life. This matter, however, is not to be reduced to any accurate rule. The determination of questions of this kind, must necessarily vary according to the circumstances of the persons concerned, and according to the temper and disposition of the actor.

The second general principle in point of rank is self-love, which, being a more powerful principle than benevolence, it naturally assumes the preference. And we meet with no obstruction from the moral sense, when we prefer our own interest to that of others.

The

LAW OF NATURE.

The same will hold with regard to our particular appetites, passions and affections. But here comes a remarkable limitation, that we are not to indulge self-love at the expence of harming others, whether in their persons, goods, or reputation. The moral sense, in every case, self-preservation excepted, lays us under an absolute restraint with regard to these particulars. This restraint is felt as our indispensible duty, and the transgression of this duty never fails to be attended with remorse, and a dread of merited punishment. And this is wisely ordered. Society could not be preserved without such a law; and even, abstracting from society, the law is essentially necessary, to attain the ends proposed by the two great principles of action, self-preservation and self-love. No man could be secure of his life a moment, far less of his happiness, if men, worse than savage beasts, preyed upon one another.

The third principle, which is that of fidelity, is also in the strictest sense a law of
nature.

nature. We are bound to take care of our children, to perform our promises, and to stand true to our engagements. It need only be observed upon this head, that the obligation is indispensible, and yields to no other principle or law of nature, if it be not self-preservation alone.

Gratitude, the fourth principle, is likeways to be ranked among the laws of nature. We feel it in the strictest sense as our duty. The transgression of this law is not only attended with self-disapprobation, but with hatred and contempt from others.

Benevolence, the last principle, may be indulged at pleasure, and without restraint, unless where it comes in competition with a strict obligation. If it is directed to advance the happiness of others; it is not to be ranked, strictly speaking, among our duties. Because, tho' actions of this kind are highly rewarded by self-approbation, and the love of others, yet the neglect of them is not attended

tended with remorse or punishment. It is true, that a person of a sociable and generous temper, will be strongly impelled to actions of this kind, and will feel pain and uneasiness upon reflecting, that he has not been so useful to his friends, his country, or mankind, as he might have been. But this uneasiness does not arise to what is properly called remorse, or self-condemnation, tho' it may, in some instances, approach to it. There is undoubtedly a distinction here, tho' it be not easy to ascertain the precise limits of feelings that are so much allied to one another, any more than it is to fix the exact boundary betwixt light and darkness, or to distinguish the very last shade of any colour in tints that run into each other. To instance in another case, which belongs to the same head of benevolence. We are obliged to provide for our children; it is strict duty, and the neglect of it causes remorse. In the case of an only brother, suppose, or some very near friend who depends entirely on our help, we feel somewhat of the same

kind

kind of obligation, tho' in a weaker degree; and thus, thro' other connections, it diminishes by succeſſive gradations, 'till at laſt the motive to benevolence is loſt in ſimple approbation, without any obligatory feeling. This is univerſally the courſe which nature holds. Her tranſitions are ſoft and gentle; ſhe makes things approximate ſo nicely one to another, as to leave no gap or chaſm. Where the object of theſe feelings can be clearly and fully diſtinguiſhed, it may be ſafely aſſerted, that, in the general caſe, of procuring poſitive good to others, or advancing happineſs, it is ſelf-approbation and not ſtrict obligation that is felt. But where the object of benevolence is diſtreſs, there it becomes a duty, provided it is in our power to afford relief without hurting ourſelves. The neglect of ſuch an action is certainly attended with remorſe and ſelf-condemnation; tho' poſſibly, not of ſo ſtrong a kind, as where we betray our truſt, or are the authors of poſitive miſchief to others. Thus
cha-

charity is, by all mankind, confidered as a duty to which we are ftrictly bound.

These are the out-lines of the laws which govern our actions, comprehending both what we *may do*, and what we *ought* to do. And now, dropping the former to be indulged by every one at pleafure without reftraint, we fhall confine ourfelves to the latter, as the more proper fubject of laws, both natural and municipal. And no more feems to be requifite in this matter, than clearly to point out our duty, by informing us of what we ought to do, and what we ought not to do; feeing actions, which come not under the character of duty, may be fafely left to our own choice. With regard then to what may be called our duty, the firft and primary law is the law of reftraint, by which we are prohibited to hurt others in their perfons, goods, or whatever elfe is dear to them. The fecond is a pofitive law, that we ought to relieve thofe in diftrefs. The omission of this duty does not, *cæteris paribus*, affect us so strongly with the sense of wrong, as the transgression does of the former law. Because the creating of positive pain has a greater effect upon the mind, than merely the forbearing to relieve others from pain; as there is a closer connection in the imagination betwixt a man and his actions, than betwixt a man and any action he forbears to do. Fidelity comes, in the third place, as a positive duty, comprehending the care of our offspring, performance of promises, executing trusts, *&c.* Gratitude takes up the fourth place of positive duty. And that branch of benevolence having for its object the advancing the good of others, takes up the last place, which, if at all to be ranked among our duties, is then only to be ranked, when it is applied to those who are nearly connected with us, and to general objects, such as our town, our religion, our government.

THESE

LAW OF NATURE.

THESE several laws are admirably adjusted to our nature and circumstances, and tend in the most perfect manner to promote the ends of society. In the first place, as man is limited with regard to power and capacity, the above laws are accommodated to his nature, ordering and forbidding nothing but what falls within his compass. In the second place, peace and security in society are amply provided for, by tying up the hands, as it were, of every man from harming others. In the third place, man is prompted to the utmost of his ability to be useful to others. 'Tis his positive duty to relieve the distressed, and perform his engagements. And he is incited to do all the good he can by the pleasure of the action, by benevolence and gratitude from the persons obliged. And lastly, in competition betwixt himself and others, tho' his principles of action directed upon himself, may be stronger than those directed upon others, the superior rewards bestowed by the constitution of our nature

upon

upon the latter, may be deemed a sufficient counter-balance to give an ascendent to the social affections.

It may seem strange, that the municipal law of all countries is so little regardful of the laws of nature, as to adopt but a very few of them. There never was a positive law in any country, to punish ingratitude, if it was not among the antient Persians. There is no positive law to enforce compassion, and to relieve those in distress, if the maintenance of the poor be excepted, which, in some countries, is provided for by law. No notice is taken of breach of friendship, by statute, nor of the duty we owe our children, further than of supporting them while they are under age. But municipal laws, being of human invention, are of no great extent. They cannot reach the heart, nor its intentions, further than as exprest by outward acts. And these are to be judged of cautiously, and with reserve; because they form a language, dark, and at best full of ambiguities. At the same time, the object of human laws is man, considered singly in the quality of a citizen. When society is formed, and government submitted to, every private right is given up, inconsistent with society and government. But, in every other respect, individuals reserve their independency and their private rights. Whether a man be virtuous, is not the concern of the society, at least not of its laws; but only whether he transgress those regulations, which are necessary to the preservation of society. In this view, great attention is given by the legislature in every country, to enforce the natural law of restraint from mutual hurt and injury. The like attention is given, to enforce the natural obligation of fidelity, at least so far as relates to commerce; for, infidelity in love and friendship are left to the natural law. Ingratitude is not punished by human laws; because it may be guarded against by positive engagements; nor

hard-

hard-heartedness with regard to objects of distress, because society may subsist without such a law; and mankind are scarce yet arrived at such refinement in manners, as to have an abhorrence of this crime, sufficient to make it an object of human punishment.

There is another substantial reason, which confines human laws within a much narrower compass, than the laws of nature. It is essential to human laws, that they be clear, plain, and readily applicable to particular cases; without which, judges would be arbitrary, and law made a handle for oppression. For this reason, none of our actions can be the object of positive law, but what are reducible to a precise rule. Ingratitude therefore cannot be the object of human laws, because the quality of the crime depends upon a multiplicity of circumstances, which can never be reduced to a precise rule. Duty to our children, friends and relations is, with regard to most circumstances, in the

same

same case. The duty of relieving the distressed, in like manner, depends upon many circumstances, the nature of the distress, the connection betwixt the parties, the opportunity and ability of affording relief. The abstinence from mutual harm, and the performance of promises are capable to be brought under a precise rule, and these only are the objects of human laws.

CHAP. IX.

Of the LAW *of* NATIONS.

IF we can truft hiftory, the original inhabitants of this earth were a brutifh and favage race. And we have little reafon to doubt of the fact, when, even at this day, we find the fame fort of people in diftant corners, who have no communication with the reft of mankind. The ftate of nature is accordingly reprefented by all writers, as a ftate of war; nothing going on but rapine and bloodfhed. From this picture of the firft men, one would be apt to conclude, that man, by nature, is a wild and rapacious animal, little better than a beaft of prey, but, for his inclination to fociety, which moulds him gradually into a rational creature. If this conclufion be juft, we cannot help being in fome pain for the principles above laid down. Brutifh manners imply brutifh principles of action; and, from this view of the original ftate of mankind, it may feem that

moral

LAW OF NATURE. 137

moral virtues are not natural, but acquired by means of education and example in a well regulated society. In a word, that the whole moral part of our system is artificial, as justice is represented by a late writer.

But to be satisfied of the fallacy of this conclusion, we need only look back to what has already been said upon the moral sense. If the feeling of beauty and deformity in external existences be natural to man, the feeling of beauty and deformity, and of a *right* and *wrong* in actions, is equally so. And indeed, whatever be the influence of education and example, 'tis an evident truth, that they can never have the power of creating any one sense or feeling. They may well have the effect of cherishing and improving the plants of nature's formation, but they cannot introduce any new or original plant whatever. We must therefore attribute the above appearances to some other cause than want of the moral sense; and these appearances may easily be accounted

for,

for, from peculiar circumſtances, that are ſufficient to over-balance the moſt vigorous operations of the moral ſenſe, and to produce, in a good meaſure, the ſame effects which would reſult from a total abſence of that ſenſe. Let us point out theſe circumſtances, for the ſubject is worthy of our ſtricteſt attention. The original ſituation of mankind will, in the firſt place, be attended to, when the earth was uncultivated, and in a great meaſure barren; when there was a ſcarcity of inſtruments for raiſing habitations, and a greater ſcarcity of manufactures to ſupply the neceſſities of life. In this ſtate, man was a moſt indigent creature, and, upon the principle of ſelf-preſervation, intitled to ſupply his wants the beſt way he could, without any obſtruction from the moral ſenſe. Thus there behoved to be a conſtant oppoſition of intereſts, and of conſequence perpetual diſcord. At the ſame time there being no eſtabliſhed rules of conduct to appeal to, nor judges to apply rules to particular caſes, wars of old behoved to be

at

LAW OF NATURE.

at least as frequent as law suits are at present. In this state, barbarity, roughness, and cruelty formed the character of the human species. For, in the practice and habit of war, the malevolent principles gain strength and vigour, as the benevolent principles, do by the arts of peace. And to this consideration may be added, that man is by nature shy and timorous, and consequently cruel when he gets the upper-hand. The security obtained in society puts an end in a great measure to our fears. Man becomes a magnanimous and generous creature, not easily daunted, and therefore not easily provoked to acts of cruelty.

It may be observed, in the next place, that the rude and illiterate are governed by their appetites and passions, more than by general principles. We have our first impressions from particular objects. 'Tis by education and practice that we acquire a facility in forming complex ideas, and abstract propositions. The ideas of a common interest,

rest, of a country, of a people, of a society under government, of publick good, are complex, and not soon acquired even by the thinking part of mankind. They are scarce ever to be acquired by the rude and illiterate; and consequently do not readily become the object of any of their affections. One's own interest, considered in general, is too complex an object for the bulk of mankind; and therefore it is, that the particular appetites and passions are stronger motives to action with the ignorant and unthinking, than the principle of self-love, or even than of self-preservation, when it is not incited by some particular object which threatens danger. And the same must hold more strongly with regard to the affections of benevolence, charity and such like, when there is no particular object in view, but only in general the good of others.

Man is a complex machine, composed of various principles of motion, which may be conceived as so many springs and weights,
coun-

counteracting and balancing one another. These being accurately adjusted, the movement of life is beautiful, because regular and uniform. But if some springs or weights be withdrawn, those which remain, acting now without opposition from their antagonist forces, will disorder the balance, and derange the whole machine. Remove those principles of action which operate by reflection, and whose objects are complex and general ideas, and the necessary consequence will be, to double the force of the appetites and passions, pointing at particular objects; which is always the case with those who act by sense, and not by reflection. They are tyrannised by passion and appetite, and have no consistent rule of conduct. No wonder, that the moral sense is of no sufficient authority to command obedience in such a case. This is the character of savages. We have no reason then to conclude, from the above picture, that even the greatest savages are destitute of the moral sense. Their defect rather lies in the weakness of their general

prin-

principles of action, which terminate in objects too complex for savages readily to comprehend. This defect is remedied by education and reflection; and then it is, that the moral sense, in concert with these general principles, acquires its full authority, which is openly recognised, and chearfully submitted to.

The contemplation is beautiful, when we compare our gradual improvement in knowledge and in morality We begin with surveying particular objects, and lay in a stock of simple ideas. Our affections keep pace, being all directed to particular objects; and, during this period, we are governed principally by our passions and appetites. So soon as we begin to form complex and general ideas, these also become the objects of our affections. Then it is, that love to our country begins to exert itself, benevolence to our neighbours and acquaintances, affection to our relations as such. We acquire by degrees the taste of public good, and of being useful in life. The pleasures of
so-

society thicken upon us. The selfish passions are tamed and subdued, and the social affections gain the ascendant. We refine upon the pleasures of society, because our happiness principally consists in social intercourse. We learn to submit our opinions. We affect to give preference to others, and readily accommodate ourselves to every thing which may render society more complete. The malevolent passions, above all, are brought under the strictest culture, if not totally eradicated. Instead of unbounded revenge for the smallest injury, we acquire a degree of self-denial to overlook trifling wrongs, and in greater wrongs to be satisfied with moderate reparation.

At the same time, it is true, that the moral sense, tho' rooted in the nature of man, admits of great refinements by culture and education. It improves gradually like our other powers and faculties, 'till it comes to be productive of the strongest as well as most delicate feelings. To clear this point, every ry one muſt be ſenſible of the great advantages of education and imitation. The moſt poliſhed nations differ only from ſavages in refinement of taſte, which, being productive of nice and delicate feelings, is the ſource of pleaſure and pain, more exquiſite than ſavages are ſuſceptible of. Hence it is, that many actions, which make little impreſſion upon ſavages, appear to us elegant and beautiful. As, on the other hand, actions, which give them no pain, raiſe in us averſion and diſguſt. This may be illuſtrated by a compariſon betwixt the Engliſh and French dramatic performances. The Engliſh, a rough and hardy people, take delight in repreſentations, which more refined manners render inſupportable to their neighbours. The diſtreſſes, on the other hand, repreſented on the French theatre, are too ſlight for an Engliſh audience. Their paſſions are not raiſed: they feel no concern. In general, horror, which denotes the higheſt degree of pain and averſion that can be raiſed by a harſh action, is a paſſion ſeldom felt among

fierce

LAW OF NATURE.

fierce and savage nations where humanity is little regarded. But, when the tender affections are improved by society, horror is more easily raised, and objects which move horror become more frequent.

The moral sense not only accompanies our other senses in their gradual refinement, but receives additional strength upon every occasion from these other senses. For example, a savage, enured to acts of cruelty, feels little pain or aversion in putting an enemy to death in cold blood, and consequently will have no remorse at such an action, other than what proceeds from the moral sense, acting by its native strength. But let us suppose a person of so delicate feelings, as scarce to endure a common operation of phlebotomy, and who cannot behold, without some degree of horror, the amputation of a fractured member; such a person will be shocked to the highest degree, if he see an enemy put to death in cold blood. The grating emotion, thus raised in him, must communicate itself to the feelings of the moral sense, and render them much more acute. And thus, refinement in taste and manners, operating by communication upon the moral sense, occasions a stronger feeling of immorality in every vicious action, than what would arise before such refinement. At the same time, the moral sense improves in its delicacy, as well as the other senses; whereby a double effect is produced, owing to a double cause. And therefore, upon the whole, the operations of the moral sense in a savage, bear no proportion to its operations in a person, who stands possessed of all the advantages which human nature is susceptible of by refined education.

I NEVER was satisfied with the description given of the law of nations, commonly so called, that it is a law established among nations by common consent, for regulating their conduct with regard to each other. This foundation of the law of nations I take to be chimerical. For, upon what occasion was

was this covenant made, and by whom? If it be said, that the sense of common good gradually brought this law into force; I answer, That the sense of common good is too complex, and too remote an object to be a solid foundation for any positive law, if it has no other foundation in our nature. But there is no necessity to recur to so slender a foundation. What is just now observed will lead us to a more rational account of these laws. They are no other but gradual refinements of the original law of nature, accommodating itself to the improved state of mankind. The law of nature, which is the law of our nature, cannot be stationary. It must vary with the nature of man, and consequently refine gradually as human nature refines. Putting an enemy to death in cold blood, is now looked upon with distaste and horror, and therefore is immoral; tho' it was not always so in the same degree. It is considered as barbarous and inhuman, to fight with poisoned weapons, and therefore is more remarkably

dis-

disapproved of by the moral sense, than it was originally. Influenced by general objects, we have enmity against France, which is our natural enemy; but this enmity is not directed against individuals; conscious as we are, that it is the duty of subjects to serve their king and country. Therefore we treat prisoners of war with humanity. And now it is creeping in among civilized nations, that, in war, a cartel should be established for exchange of prisoners. The function of an embassador has ever been held sacred. To treat him ill was originally immoral, because it is treating as an enemy the man who comes to us with friendly intentions. But the improved manners of latter times, have refined upon the privileges of an embassador, and extended them far beyond what they were originally. It is very true, that these refinements of the law of nature gain strength and firmness by custom. Hereby they acquire the additional support of common consent. For, as every nation trusts that these laws will be observed, it is

upon

upon that account a breach of faith to transgress them. But this is not peculiar to these particular institutions which pass under the name of the law of nations. There is the same adventitious foundation for all the laws of nature, which every man trusts will be observed, and upon that faith directs his conduct.

ESSAY

ESSAY III.

Of LIBERTY *and* NECESSITY.

WHEN we apply our thoughts to the contemplation of final causes, no subject more readily presents itself than the natural world, which is stamped with the brightest characters of wisdom and goodness. The moral world, being less in view, has been generally overlooked, tho' it yields not to the other in rich materials. Man's inward system, accurately surveyed, will be found not less admirable than the external system, of which he makes a part. The subject is the more curious, that the traces of wisdom and design, discernible in our internal frame, ly more out of common sight. They are touches, as it were, of a finer pencil, and of a nicer hand, than are discovered in the natural world. Thought is more subtile than motion, and more of exquisite art is displayed in the laws of voluntary ac-

tion,

tion, than there is place for in adjusting the laws of mere matter.

An extreme beautiful scene opens to our view, when we consider with what propriety the ideas, feelings, and whole constitution of the mind of man, correspond to his present state. The impressions he receives, and the notions he forms, are accurately adapted to the useful purposes of life, tho' they do not correspond in every instance to the philosophic truth of things. It was not intended that man should make profound discoveries. He is framed to be more an active than a contemplative being; and his views both of the natural and moral world are so adjusted, as to be made subservient to correctness of action rather than of belief. Several instances there are of perceptions, which, for want of a more proper term, may be called deceitful; because they differ from the real truth. But man is not thereby in the least misled. On the contrary, the ends of life and action are better provided

vided for by such artifice, than if these perceptions were more exact copies of their objects.

In the natural world, somewhat of this kind is generally admitted by modern philosophers. It is found, that the representations of external objects, and their qualities conveyed by the senses, sometimes differ from what philosophy discovers these objects, and their qualities to be. Thus a surface appears smooth and uniform, when its roughness is not such as to be hurtful. The same surface, examined with a microscope, is found to be full of ridges and hollows. Were man endowed with a microscopic eye, the bodies that surround him, would appear as different from what they do at present, as if he were transported into another world. His ideas, upon that supposition, would indeed be more agreeable to strict truth, but they would be far less serviceable in common life. Further, it is now universally admitted, that the qualities called secundary,

which

which we by natural inſtinct attribute to matter, belong not properly to matter, nor exiſt really without us. Colour in particular is a ſort of viſionary beauty, which nature has ſpread over all her works. It is a wonderful artifice, to preſent objects to us thus differently diſtinguiſhed: to mark them out to the eye in various attires, ſo as to be beſt known and remembered: and to paint on the fancy, gay and lively, grand and ſtriking, or ſober and melancholy ſcenes: whence many of our moſt pleaſurable and moſt affecting ſenſations ariſe. Yet all this beauty of colours, with which heaven and earth appear clothed, is a ſort of romance and illuſion. For, among external objects, to which colours are attributed by ſenſe, there is really no other diſtinction, than what ariſes from a difference in the ſize and arrangement of the conſtituent parts, whereby the rays of light, are reflected or refracted in ſuch different ways, as to paint various colours on the retina of the eye. From this, and other inſtances of the ſame kind which might be adduced, it appears, that

that our perceptions fome times, are lefs accommodated to the truth of things, than to the end for which our fenfes are defigned. Nature, at the fame time, has provided a remedy; for fhe feldom or never leaves us without means of difcovering the deception, and arriving at the truth. And it is wonderful, that, even when we act upon thefe deceitful impreffions, we are not betrayed into any thing that is hurtful. On the contrary, life and action are better provided for, and the ends of our being fulfilled to more advantage, than if we conducted ourfelves by the ftricteft truth of things.

Let us carry on this fpeculation from the natural to the moral world, and examine whether there are not here alfo, analogous inftances of deceitful impreffions. This will lead us into an unbeaten tract. We are to open a fcene entirely new; which, like moft other things that are new, may perhaps furprize the reader. But he will fufpend his judgment, 'till he has leifurely reviewed the

the whole: and then let him pronounce, whether our hypothesis does not solve all the phœnomena: whether it does not tally with the nature of man, and illustrate the wisdom and goodness of the author of his nature.

That nothing can happen without a cause, is a principle embraced by all men, the illiterate and ignorant as well as the learned. Nothing that happens is conceived as happening of itself, but as an *effect* produced by some other thing. However ignorant of the cause, we notwithstanding conclude, that every event must have a cause. We should perhaps be at a loss to deduce this principle, from any premises, by a chain of reasoning: but feeling affords conviction, where reason leaves us in the dark. We perceive, we feel the proposition to be true. And, indeed, a sentiment, common to all, must be founded on the common nature of all. Curiosity is one of the earliest passions that are discovered in children; and their curiosity

curiosity runs on nothing more than to have causes and reasons given them, why such a thing happened, or how it came about. Historians and politicians make it their chief concern, to trace the causes, of actions, the most mysterious not excepted. Be an event ever so extraordinary, the feeling of its being an effect, is not in the least weakened, even with the vulgar, who, rather than assign no cause, recur to the operation of invisible powers. What is a cause with respect to its proper effect, is considered as an effect with respect to some prior cause, and so backward without end. Events thus viewed, in a train of causes and effects, should naturally be considered, one would think, as necessary and fixed: for the relation betwixt a cause and its effect implies somewhat precise and determinate, and leads our thoughts to what must be, and cannot be otherways than it is.

That we have such a feeling as is above described, is not to be controverted: and yet,

yet, when we search further into human nature, a feeling of an opposite kind is discovered, a feeling of chance or contingency in events; which is not less deeply rooted in our nature than the former. However strange it may appear, that man should be composed of such inconsistencies, the fact must notwithstanding be admitted. This feeling of chance or contingency is most conspicuous, when we look forward to future events. Some things we indeed always consider, as certain or necessary, such as the revolution of seasons, and the rising and setting of the sun. These, as experience teaches, are regulated by fixed laws. But many things appear to us loose, fortuitous, uncertain. Uncertain not only with respect to us, on account of our ignorance of the cause, but uncertain in themselves, or not tied down, and predetermined to fall out, by any invariable law. We naturally make a distinction betwixt things that *must be*, and things that *may be*, or *may not be*. Thus we have a feeling of chance or of contingency in events, in which

that

that other feeling, of the dependency of events upon precise and determinate causes, appears to be lost.

When we consider in what view our own actions are perceived by the mind, there is something which is equally strange and surprising. It is admitted by all men, that we act from motives. The plain man, as well as the philosopher, feels the connection betwixt an action and its motive, to be so strong, that, from this feeling, both of them reason with full confidence about the future actions of others. That an avaritious man, will take every fair opportunity of acquiring riches, is as little doubted, as that rain and sun-shine will make plants grow. Why, but because the motive of gain, is judged to operate, as certainly and infallibly, upon his temper, as heat and moisture upon the soil, each to produce its proper effect? If we are uncertain what part a man will act, the uncertainty arises, not from our doubting whether he will act from a motive;

tive; for this is never called in question: it arises from our not being able to judge, what the motive is, which, in his present circumstances, will prevail. It being then a natural feeling, that actions are so connected with their proper motives, as necessarily to arise from the temper, character, and other circumstances of the agent, it should seem, that all the train of human actions, would occur to our minds as necessary and fixed. Yet human actions do not always appear to us in this light. It is a matter of fact, that the feeling varies, according to the different positions of the object. Previous to any particular action, we indeed always judge, that the action will be the necessary result of some motive. But has a man done what is wrong and shameful? Instantly the feeling varies. We accuse, and we condemn him, for acting the wrong and shameful part. We conceive that he had a power of acting otherways, and *ought* to have acted otherways. The whole train of our feelings, in a moment, accommodate themselves to

the

the fuppofition of his being entirely a free agent.

THESE are phænomena in human nature, of a very fingular kind: feelings, which on both fides are natural, and yet clafh with each other: every event admitted to have a neceffary caufe; and yet many events fuppofed contingent: every action admitted neceffarily to flow from a determining motive; and yet the fame action, in an after view, confidered and judged of as free. Our feelings are no doubt the teft of truth; which is fo evident, that, in many inftances, no other means are afforded us for coming at the truth. The few exceptions that are difcovered by reafon or experience, ferve the more to confirm the general rule. But the feelings we have now laid open can be no teft of truth; becaufe, in contradictory propofitions, truth cannot ly on both fides. There is no other way to get out of this labyrinth of doubts and difficulties, than to enter upon a ftrict furvey both of the natural

ral and moral world, which may possibly lead to a discovery of what is really the truth of the matter. Let us then proceed, with impartiality and attention, to inquire what we are to believe, concerning contingency in events, and liberty or necessity in human actions: whether our feelings can be reconciled to each other, and reconciled to truth; or whether there be not here some of those deceitful feelings, which we have already hinted in some other instances to belong to our nature.

TAKING a view of the natural world, we find all things there proceeding in a fixed and settled train of causes and effects. It is a point which admits of no dispute, that all the changes produced in matter, and all the different modifications it assumes, are the result of fixed laws. Every effect is so precisely determined, that no other effect could, in such circumstances, have possibly resulted from the operation of the cause: which holds even in the minutest changes of the dif-

different elements, as all philosophers admit. Casual and fluctuatiug as these seem, their smallest variation is a necessary effect of pre-established laws. There is a chain of causes and effects which hang one upon another, running thro' this whole system; and not the smallest link of the chain can be broken, without altering the whole constitution of things, or suspending the regular operation of the laws of nature. Here then, in the material world, there is nothing that can be called *contingent*; nothing that is left loose; but every thing must be precisely what it is, and be found in that state in which we find it.

In the moral world, this does not appear so clearly. Man is the actor here. He is endowed with will, and he acts from choice. He has a power of beginning motion, which is subject to no mechanical laws; and therefore he is not under what is called physical necessity. He has appetites and passions which prompt him to their respective gratifications:

cations: but he is under no necessity of blindly submitting to their impulse. For reason has a power of restraint. It suggests motives from the cool views of good and evil. He deliberates upon these. In consequence of his deliberation he chuses: and here, if anywhere, lyes our liberty. Let us examine to what this liberty amounts. That motives have some influence in determining the mind, is certain; and that they have this influence in different degrees, is equally certain. The sense of honour and gratitude, for instance, are powerful motives to serve a friend. Let the man's private interest concur; and the motives become more powerful. Add the certain prospect of poverty, shame, or bodily suffering, if he shall act a different part; and you leave him no choice: the motives to action are rendered irresistible. Motives being once allowed to have a determining force in any degree, it is easy to suppose the force so augmented, by accumulation of motives, as to leave little freedom to the mind, or rather none at all. In
such

such instances, there is no denying that we are under a necessity to act. And tho' this, to be sure, is not physical necessity, as arising not from the laws of matter, but from the constitution of the mind; yet the consequence is equally certain, fixed and unavoidable, in the case of moral, as of physical necessity. This is so true, that, in some instances, these two kinds of necessity seem to coincide, so as scarcely to be distinguished. A criminal walks to the scaffold in the midst of his guards. No man will deny that he is under an absolute necessity in this case. Why? because he knows, that if he refuses to go, they will drag him. I ask, Is this a physical, or a moral necessity? The answer, at first view, is not obvious; for the distinction betwixt these two seems lost. And yet, strictly speaking, it is only a moral necessity: for it is the force of a motive which determines the criminal to walk to the scaffold; to wit, that resistance is vain, because the guards are neither to be forced nor corrupted. The idea of necessity, however,

ver, in the minds of the spectators, when they view the criminal in this situation, is not less strong, than if they saw him bound and carried on a sledge. Nothing is more common, than to talk of an action which one must do, and cannot avoid. He was compelled to it, we say; and it was impossible he could act otherways: when, at the same time, all the compulsion we mean, is only the application of some very strong motive to the mind. This shows, that, in the judgment and feeling of all mankind, a motive may, in certain circumstances, carry in it the power of rendering an action necessary. In other words, we expect such an action in consequence of such a motive, with equal confidence, as when we expect to see a stone fall to the ground when it is dropt from the hand.

This, it will be said, may hold in some instances, but not in all. For, in the greater part of human actions, there is a real feeling of liberty. When the mind hesitates betwixt

two

two things, examines and compares, and at last comes to a resolution, is there any compulsion or necessity here? No compulsion, it is granted; but as to necessity, let us pause and examine more accurately. The resolution being taken, the choice being made, upon what is it founded? Certainly upon some motive, however silent or weak: for no mortal ever came to a determination, without the influence of some motive or other. If this be an undoubted fact, it follows of consequence, that the determination must result, from that motive, which has the greatest influence for the time; or from what appears the best and most eligible upon the whole. If motives be of very different kinds, with regard to strength and influence, which we feel to be the case; it is involved in the very idea of the strongest motive, that it must have the strongest effect in determining the mind. This can no more be doubted of, than that, in a balance, the greater weight must turn the scale.

HERE

Here perhaps we shall be interrupted. Men are not always rational in their determinations: they often act from whim, paffion, humour, things as loofe and variable as the wind. This is admitted. But, fuppofe the motive which determines the mind, to be as whimfical and unreafonable as you pleafe, its influence, however, is equally neceffary with that of the moft rational motive. An indolent man, for inftance, is incited to action, by the ftrongeft confiderations, which reafon, virtue, intereft, can fuggeft. He wavers and hefitates; at laft refifts them all, and folds his arms. What is the caufe of this? Is it that he is lefs under the power of motives than another man? By no means. The love of reft is his motive, his prevailing paffion: and this is as effectual to fix him in his place, as the love of glory or riches are, to render active, the vain or the covetous. In fhort, if motives are not under our power or direction, which is confeffedly the fact, we can, at bottom, have no liberty. We are fo conftituted, that we cannot exert a fingle action,

action, but with some view, aim or purpose. At the same time, when two opposite motives present themselves, we have not the power of an arbitrary choice. We are directed, by a necessary determination of our nature, to prefer the strongest motive.

It is true, that, in disputing upon this subject of human liberty, a man may attempt to show, that motives have no necessary influence, by eating perhaps the worst apple that is before him, or, in some such trifling instance, preferring an obviously lesser good to a greater. But is it not plain, that the humour of showing that he can act against motives, is, in this case, the very motive of the whimsical preference?

A comparison instituted betwixt moral and physical necessity may possibly throw additional light upon this subject. Where the motives to any action are perfectly full, cogent and clear, the feeling of liberty, as we showed before, entirely vanishes. In

other

other cases, where the field of choice is wider, and where opposite motives counterbalance and work against each other, the mind fluctuates for a while, and feels itself more loose: but, in the end, must as necessarily be determined to the side of the most powerful motive, as the balance, after several vibrations, must incline to the side of the preponderating weight. The laws of mind, and the laws of matter, are in this respect perfectly similar; tho', in making the comparison, we are apt to deceive ourselves. In forming a notion of physical necessity, we seldom think of any force, but what has visibly a full effect. A man in prison, or tied to a post, must remain there. If he is dragged along, he cannot resist. Whereas motives, which, from the highest to the lowest, are very different, do not always produce sensible effects. Yet, when the comparison is accurately instituted, the very same thing holds in the actions of matter. A weak motive makes some impression: but, in opposition to one more powerful, it has no effect

to

to determine the mind. In the precise same manner, a small force will not overcome a great resistance; nor the weight of an ounce in one scale, counter-balance a pound in the other. Comparing together the actions of mind and matter, similar causes will, in both equally, produce similar effects.

But admitting all that has been contended for, of the necessary influence of motives, to bring on the choice or last judgment of the understanding, it is urged by Dr. *Clark*, that man is still a free agent, because he has a power of acting, or beginning motion according to his will. In this, he places human liberty, that motives are not physical efficient causes of motion *. We agree with the doctor, that the immediate efficient cause of motion is not the motive, but the will to act. No person ever held, that the pleasure of a summer-evening, when a man goes abroad into the fields, is

the

---

* Vid. demonstration of the being and attributes, p. 565. fol. edit. and his answer to Colin's passim.

the immediate cauſe of the motion of his feet. But what does this obſervation avail, when the prevailing motive, the will to act, and the action itſelf, are three things inſeparably linked together? The motive, according to his own conceſſion, neceſſarily determines the will; and the will neceſſarily produces the action, unleſs it be obſtructed by ſome foreign force. Is not the action, by conſequence, as neceſſary, as the will to act; tho' the motive be the immediate cauſe of the will only, and not of the action or beginning of motion? What does this author gain, by ſhowing, that we have a power of beginning motion, if that power never is, never can be, exerted, unleſs in conſequence of ſome volition or choice, which is neceſſarily cauſed? But, ſays he, it is only a moral neceſſity which is produced by motives; and a moral neceſſity, he adds, is no neceſſity at all, but is conſiſtent with the higheſt liberty. If theſe words have any meaning, the diſpute is at an end. For moral neceſſity, being that ſort of neceſſity which affects the mind,

and

and physical necessity that which affects matter, it is plain, that, in all reasonings concerning human liberty, moral necessity, and no other, is meant to be established. The laws of action, we say, which respect the human mind, are as fixed as those which respect matter. The different nature of these laws, occasions the fixed consequences of the one to be called moral, and of the other to be called physical necessity. But the idea of *necessary, certain, unavoidable*, equally agrees to both. And to say that moral necessity is no necessity at all, because it is not physical necessity, which is all that the doctor's argument amounts to, is no better, than to argue, that physical necessity is no necessity at all, because it is not moral necessity.

One great source of confusion, in reflecting upon this subject, seems to be, our not distinguishing betwixt necessity and constraint. In common language, these are used as equivalent terms; but they ought to be distinguished when we treat of this subject. A person, having a strong desire to escape,

remains

remains in prison, because the doors are guarded. Finding his keepers gone, he makes his escape. His escape now is as necessary, *i. e.* as certain and infallible a consequence of the circumstances he finds himself in, as his confinement was before; tho', in the one case there is constraint, in the other none. In this lyes the liberty of our actions, in being free from constraint, and in acting according to our inclination and choice. But as this inclination and choice is unavoidably caused or occasioned by the prevailing motive; in this lyes the necessity of our actions, that, in such circumstances, it was impossible we could act otherways. In this sense all our actions are equally necessary.

The preceeding reasonings may perhaps make a stronger impression, by being reduced into a short argument, after this manner. No man can be conceived to act without some principle leading him to action. All our principles of action resolve into *desires* and *aversions*; for nothing can prompt us to

move

move or exert ourselves in any shape, but what presents some object to be either pursued or avoided. A motive is an object so operating upon the mind, as to produce either desire or aversion. Now, liberty as opposed to moral necessity, must signify a power in the mind, of acting without or against motives; that is to say, a power of acting without any view, purpose or design, and even of acting in contradiction to our own desires and aversions, or to all our principles of action; which power, besides that no man was ever conscious of it, seems to be an absurdity altogether inconsistent with a rational nature.

With regard to things supposed so equal as to found no preference of one to another, it is not necessary to enter into any intricate inquiry, how the mind in such cases is directed. Tho' it should be admitted, that where there is no sort of motive to influence the mind, it may exert a power of acting arbitrarily, this would not affect the preceeding

ceeding reasonings, in which, the existence of a motive being once supposed, we have shown the mind to be necessarily determined. Objects, so balanced one against another with perfect equality, if such instances are to be found, must be so few, and in matters so trivial (as in the common instance of eggs) that they can have very inconsiderable influence upon human life. It may well admit of a doubt, whether the mind be, in any case, left altogether destitute of a motive to determine its choice betwixt two objects. For, tho' the objects should be themselves perfectly equal, yet various circumstances arising from minute unobserved specialities, of fancy, custom, proximity of place, &c. may turn the scale in favours of one of the objects, to make it the motive of election. The uneasiness one is conscious of, when in this state of suspense, betwixt two things equally balanced, searching and casting about for some ground of choice; this uneasiness, I say, sufficiently shows, that to act altogether

ar-

arbitrary is unnatural, and that our constitution fits us to be determined by motives.

But now a thought comes across the mind, which demands attention. How hard is the lot of the human species, to be thus tied down and fixed to motives; subjected by a necessary law to the choice of evil, if evil happen to be the prevailing motive, or if it mislead us under the form of our greatest interest or good! How happy to have had a free independent power of acting contrary to motives, when the prevailing motive has a bad tendency! By this power, we might have pushed our way to virtue and happiness, whatever motives were suggested by vice and folly to draw us back; or we might, by arbitrary will, have refrained from acting the bad part, tho' all the power of motives concurred to urge us on. So far well; but let us see whither this will carry us. This arbitrary power being once supposed, may it not be exerted against good motives as well as bad ones? If it does us good by accident, in restraining us from vice, may it not do us ill by accident, in restraining us from virtue? and so shall we not be thrown loose altogether? At this rate, no man could be depended upon. Promises, oaths, vows, would be in vain; for nothing can ever bind or fix a man who is influenced by no motive. The distinction of characters would be at an end; for a person cannot have a character, who has no fixed or uniform principles of action. Nay, moral virtue itself, and all the force of law, rule and obligation, would, upon this hypothesis, be nothing. For no creature can be the subject of rational or moral government, whose actions, by the constitution of its nature, are independent of motives; and whose will is capricious and arbitrary. To exhort, to instruct, to promise, or to threaten, would be to no purpose. In short, such a creature, if such could exist, would be a most bizarre and unaccountable being: a mere absurdity in nature, whose existence could serve no end. Were we so constituted, as

always

always to be determined by the moral sense, even against the strongest counter-motives, this would be consistent with human nature, because it would preserve entire the connection, that, by an unalterable law, is established betwixt the will and the prevailing motive. But, to break this connection altogether, to introduce an unbounded arbitrary liberty, in opposition to which, motives should not have influence, would be, instead of amending, to deform and unhinge the whole human constitution. No reason have we therefore to regret, that we find the will necessarily subjected to motives. The truth of this general position must coincide with our wish, unless we would rather have man to be, a whimsical and ridiculous, than a rational and moral being.

Thus far then we have advanced in our argument, that all human actions proceed in a fixed and necessary train. Man being what he is, a creature endowed with a certain degree of understanding, certain passions

ons and principles, and placed in certain circumstances, it is impossible he should will or chuse otherways, than in fact he wills or chuses. His mind is passive in receiving impressions of things as good or ill: according to these impressions, the last judgment of the understanding is necessarily formed; which the will, if considered as different from the last judgment of the understanding, necessarily obeys, as is fully shown; and the external action is necessarily connected with the will, or the mind's final determination to act.

In the course of this reasoning, we have abstracted from all controversies about Divine Prescience and Decree. Tho' in fact, from what has been proved, it appears, that the Divine Being decrees all future events. For he who gave such a nature to his creatures, and placed them in such circumstances, that a certain train of actions behoved necessarily to follow; he, I say, who did so, and who must have foreseen the consequences,

quences, did certainly resolve or decree that events should fall out, and men should act as they do. Prescience indeed is not, properly speaking, any cause of events. For events do not happen, because they are foreseen; but because they are certainly to happen, therefore they are capable of being foreseen. Tho' prescience does not cause, yet it undoubtedly supposes, the certain futurition (as schoolmen speak) of events. And, were there not causes which render the existence of future events certain, it would involve a contradiction to maintain, that future events could be certainly foreseen. But I avoid carrying the reader any further into such thorny disputes.

The sum of what we have discovered concerning contingency in events, and liberty in actions is this. Comparing together the moral and the natural world, every thing is as much the result of established laws in the one as in the other. There is nothing in the whole universe that can properly be
called

called contingent, that may be, or may not be; nothing loose and fluctuating in any part of nature; but every motion in the natural, and every determination and action in the moral world, are directed by immutable laws: so that, whilst these laws remain in their force, not the smallest link of the universal chain of causes and effects can be broken, nor any one thing be otherways than it is *.

THE

---

* As to an objection of making God the author of sin, which may seem to arise from our system, it is rather popular than philosophical. Sin, or moral turpitude, lyes in the evil intention of him who commits it: it consists in some wrong or depraved affection supposed to be in the sinner. Now the intention of the Deity is unerringly good. The end proposed by him is order and general happiness: and there is the greatest reason to believe, that all events are so directed by him, as to work towards this end. In the present system of things, some moral disorders are indeed included. No doubt, it is a considerable difficulty, how evil comes to be in the world, if God is perfectly good. But this difficulty is not peculiar to our doctrine; but recurs upon us at last with equal force, whatever hypothesis we embrace. For moral evil cannot exist, without being, at least, permitted by the Deity. And, with regard to a first cause, PERMITTING is the same thing with CAUSING; since, against his will nothing can possibly happen. All the schemes

that

The doctrine of universal necessity being thus laid fairly open, and proved to be the true system of the universe; we return to take a more deliberate view of the feelings of contingency and liberty, than was necessary in broaching the subject. And, as we must now admit, perhaps reluctantly, that these feelings are in reality of the delusive kind, our next and only remaining theme will be to unravel, if possible, this curious mystery, by trying to reach the purpose of endowing man with feelings, so contradictory to the truth of things.

And to begin with a review of the feeling of contingency. It is certain, that, in our ordinary train of thinking, things never occur to us in the light above set forth. A multitude of events appear to us as depending upon ourselves to cause or to prevent: and we readily make a distinction betwixt events, which are necessary, *i. e.* which must be, and events which are contingent, *i. e.* which may be,

that have been contrived for answering this objection, are but the tortoise introduced to support the elephant. They put the difficulty a step further off, but never remove it.

be, or may not be. This diftinction is without foundation in truth: for all things that fall out, either in the natural or moral world, are, as we have feen, alike neceffary, and alike the refult of fixed laws. Yet, how much foever a philofopher may be convinced of this, the diftinction betwixt things neceffary, and things contingent, remains as much with him, in the common train of his thoughts, as with any other man. We act univerfally upon this fuppofed diftinction. Nay, it is in truth the foundation of all the labour, care and induftry of mankind. To illuftrate this by an example; conftant experience has taught us, that death is a neceffary event. The human frame is not made to laft, as it is, for ever; and therefore no man thinks of acquiring a natural immortality. But the particular time of our death appears a contingent event. However certain it be, that the precife time and manner of each man's death, is determined by a train of precceding caufes, not lefs neceffary than the hour of the fun's rifing or fetting

to-

to-morrow, yet no person is in the least affected by this doctrine. In the care of prolonging life, every man is conducted by the feeling he has, of the contingency of the time of his death; which, to a certain term of years, he considers as depending in a great measure upon himself, by caution against accidents, due use of exercise, medicine, &c. To these means, he applies himself with the same diligence, as if there was, in fact, no necessary train of causes, to fix the period of his life. In short, whoever attends to his own practical ideas; whoever reflects upon the meaning of these words, which occur in all languages, of things *possible, contingent, that are in our power to cause or prevent*; whoever, I say, reflects upon such words, will clearly see, that they suggest certain feelings, or natural notions, repugnant to the doctrine above established, of universal necessity *.

* This repugnancy of feeling to truth, gave rise to the famous dispute concerning things possible, among the antient Stoicks, who held this doctrine of universal necessity. Diodorus

What then shall be done in this case, where truth contradicts the common feelings and natural notions of mankind; where it presents to us, with irresistible evidence, a system of universal necessity upon which we never act; but are so formed, as to conduct our-

---

dorus, as Cicero informs us in his book *de fato*, cap. vii. held this opinion, " Id solum fieri posse, quod aut verum " sit, aut futurum sit verum; at quicquid futurum sit, id di- " cit fieri necesse esse, et quicquid non sit futurum, id ne- " gat fieri posse." That is, he maintained, there is nothing contingent in future events, nothing possible to happen, but that precise event which will happen. This no doubt was carrying their system its due length: tho', in this way of speaking, there is something that manifestly shocks the natural feelings of mankind. Chrysippus, on the other hand, sensible of the harshness of the above consequence, maintained, that it is possible for future events to happen otherways than in fact they happen. In this, he was certainly inconsistent with his general system of necessity; and therefore, as Cicero gives us to understand, was often embarassed in the dispute with Diodorus: and Plutarch, in his book, *de repugnantiis Stoicorum*, exposes him for this inconsistency. But Chrysippus chose to follow his natural feelings, in opposition to philosophy; holding by this, that Diodorus's doctrine of nothing being possible but what happens, was *ignava ratio*, tending to absolute inaction; *cui si pareamus*, as Cicero expresses it, *nihil omnino agamus in vita*. So early were philosophers sensible of the difficulty of reconciling speculation with feeling, as to this doctrine of fate.

ourselves by a system of notions quite opposite? Shall we sacrifice abstract truth to feeling? or shall we stand by truth, and force our feelings into compliance? Neither of these will do. Truth is too rigid to bend to mere feeling; and our feelings are incapable of being forced by speculation. The attempt is vain, *pugnantia secum, frontibus adversis, componere.* Let us be honest then. Let us fairly own, that the truth of things is on the side of necessity; but that it was necessary for man to be formed, with such feelings and notions of contingency, as would fit him for the part he has to act. This thought requires illustration.

THE Deity is the first cause of all things. He formed, in his infinite mind, the great plan or scheme, upon which all things were to be governed; and put it in execution, by establishing certain laws, both in the natural and moral world, which are fixed and immutable. By virtue of these laws, all things proceed in a regular train of causes and effects,

fects, bringing about those events which are comprehended in the original plan, and admitting the possibility of none other. This universe is a vast machine, winded up and set a going. The several springs and wheels act unerringly one upon another. The hand advances, and the clock strikes, precisely as the artist has determined. Whoever has just ideas, and a true taste of philosophy, will see this to be the real theory, of the universe; and that, upon any other theory, there can be no general order, no whole, no plan, no means nor end in its administration. In this plan, man, a rational creature, was to bear his part, and to fulfill certain ends, for which he was designed. He was to appear as an actor, and to act with consciousness and spontaneity. He was to exercise thought and reason, and to receive the improvements of his nature, by the due use of these rational powers. Consequently it was necessary, that he should have some idea of liberty; some feeling of things possible and contingent, things depending upon him-

himself to cause, that he might be led to a proper exercise of that activity, for which he was designed. To have had his instinctive feelings, his practical ideas, formed upon the scheme of universal necessity; to have seen himself a part of that great machine, winded up, and set a going, by the author of his nature, would have been altogether incongruous to the ends he was to fulfill. Then, indeed, the *ignava ratio*, the inactive doctrine of the Stoicks, would have followed. Conceiving nothing to be contingent, or depending upon himself to cause, there would have been no room for fore-thought about futurity, nor for any sort of industry and care: he would have had no motives to action, but immediate sensations of pleasure and pain. He must have been formed like the brutes, who have no other principle of action, but mere instinct. The few instincts he is at present endowed with, would have been altogether insufficient. He must have had an instinct to sow, another to reap. He must have had instincts to pursue every con-

ve-

veniency, and perform every office of life. In short, reason and thought could not have been exercised in the way they are, that is, man could not have been man, had he not been furnished with a feeling of contingency. In this, as in all things else, the Divine Wisdom and Goodness are most admirable. As, in the natural world, the Almighty has adapted our senses, not to the discovery of the intimate nature and essences of things, but to the uses and conveniencies of life; as he has, in several instances, exhibited natural objects to us, not in their real, but in a sort of artificial view, clothed with such distinctions, and producing such sensations as are for the benefit of man: so he has exhibited the intellectual world to us, in a like artificial view, clothed with certain colours and distinctions, imaginary, but useful. Life is conducted according to this artificial view of things, and, by our speculations, is not in the least affected. Let the philosopher meditate in his closet upon abstract truth; let him be ever

so

so much convinced of the settled, necessary, train of causes and effects, which leaves nothing, properly speaking, in his power; yet, the moment he comes forth into the world, he acts as a free agent. And, what is wonderful, tho' in this he acts upon a false supposition, yet he is not thereby misled from the ends of action, but, on the contrary, fulfills them, to the best advantage. Long experience has made him sensible, that some things, such as the sun's rising and setting, depend upon immutable laws. This is contradicted by no feeling, as it is no way for his benefit, that he should act upon any other supposition, Such things he reckons upon as necessary. But there are other things, which depend upon the spontaneous choices of men, or upon a concurrence of natural and moral causes. As to these, he has not knowledge enough, to foresee and determine by what law they will happen: and his ignorance of the event, is made to have the same effect upon his mind, as if the event were what we vulgarly call contingent.

gent. Its *uncertainty as to him* produces the same feeling, and stirs him up to the same activity, as if it were *uncertain in itself*, and had no determined cause of its futurition. This feeling then of contingency, and all the ideas connected with it, may be treated as secondary qualities, which have no real existence in things; but, like other secondary qualities, are made to appear as existing in events, or belonging to them, in order to serve the necessary purposes of human life.

Some objections shall be considered, after discussing the other branch of the disquisition concerning liberty of action. These subjects are so closely connected, that they cannot fail to throw light upon each other. Contingency in events is analogous to liberty in actions. The one is a supposed quality of the thing; the other of the actor.

The extent of human liberty is above ascertained. It consists in spontaneity, or acting according to our inclination and choice.

It

It may be therefore diftinguifhed from *conftraint*, but muft not be oppofed to neceffity. For, as has been fully fhown, the mind, in the moft calm choice, the moft deliberate action, is neceffarily, *i. e.* unavoidably and certainly, determined by the prepollent motive. When we examine accurately, how far our feelings correfpond to this fyftem; we find, as was hinted before, firft, that, antecedent to any particular action, we generally think and reafon upon the fcheme of neceffity. In confidering or gueffing at future events, we always conclude, that a man will act confiftently with his character; we infer what his actions will be, from the knowledge we have of his temper, and the motives that are fitted to influence it; and never dream of any man's having a power of acting againft motives. Here we have a very weak feeling, if any at all, of liberty, as diftinguifhed from neceffity: and wifely fo ordered, that a clue, as it were, might be afforded, to guide us in the labyrinth of future actions, which, were it not for the connection betwixt an action and its motive, would appear like a rope of sand, loose and unconnected; and no means left of reasoning upon, or foreseeing future actions. It is to be observed in the next place, that, during the action, the feeling begins to vary; and, unless in cases where the motive is so strong and overbearing, as to approach to the nature of constraint; unless, in these, a man has a feeling of liberty, or of a power of acting otherways than he is doing. But, in the third place, it is principally in reflecting and passing judgment upon a past action, that the feeling of liberty is sensible and strong. Then it is, that our actions are not considered as proceeding in a necessary unavoidable train: but we accuse and blame others, for not having acted the part they *might* and *ought* to have acted, and condemn ourselves, and feel remorse, for having been guilty of a wrong we *might have* refrained from. The operations of moral conscience plainly proceed upon this supposition, that there is such a power in man of directing

his

his actions, as rendered it possible for the person accused, to have acted a better part. This affords an argument, which the advocates for liberty have urged in its full force, against the doctrine of necessity. They reason thus: If actions be necessary, and not in our own power, and if we know it to be so, what ground can there be for reprehension and blame, for self-condemnation and remorse? If a clock had understanding to be sensible of its own motions, knowing, at the same time, that they proceed according to necessary laws, could it find fault with itself for striking wrong? Would it not blame the artist, who had ill adjusted the wheels on which its movements depended? So that, upon this scheme, say they, all the moral constitution of our nature is overturned. There is an end to all the operations of conscience about right and wrong. Man is no longer a moral agent, nor the subject of praise or blame for what he does.

THIS

This difficulty is great, and never has been surmounted by the advocates for necessity. They endeavour to surmount it, by reconciling feeling to philosophic truth, in the following manner. We are so constituted, they say, that certain affections, and the actions which proceed from them, appear odious and base; and others agreeable and lovely; that, wherever they are beheld, either in ourselves or others, the moral sense necessarily approves of the one, and condemns the other; that this approbation is immediate and instinctive, without any reflection on the liberty or necessity of actions; that, on the contrary, the more any person is under the power of his affections and passions, and, by consequence, the greater necessity he is under, the more virtuous or vicious he is esteemed.

But this account of the matter is not satisfactory. All that is here said, is in the main true, but is not the whole truth. I appeal to any man who has been guilty of a bad action, which gives him uneasiness, whether

ther there is not somewhat more in the inward feeling, than merely a dislike or disapprobation of the affection, from which his action proceeded? whether the pain, the *cruciatus* of remorse, is not founded on the notion of a power he has over his will and actions, that he might have forborn to do the ill thing? and whether it is not upon this account, that he is galled within, angry at himself, and confesses himself to be justly blameable? An uneasiness somewhat of the same kind, is felt upon the reflection of any foolish or rash action, committed against the rules of wisdom. The sting is indeed much sharper, and for very wise reasons, when a man has trespassed against the rules of strict morality. But, in both cases, the uneasiness proceeds upon the supposition, that he was free, and had it in his power to have acted a better part. This indeed is true, that to be so entirely under the power of any bad passion, (lust, for instance, or cruelty) as to be incapable of acting otherways than they direct, constitutes

a vea very hateful character. I admit, that all such ill affections are naturally, and in themselves, the objects of dislike and hatred, wherever they are beheld. But I insist upon it, that mere dislike and hatred, are not the whole, but only a part of the moral feeling. The person, thus under the dominion of bad passions, is accused, is condemned, singly upon this ground, that it was *thro' his own fault* he became so subject to them; in other words, that it was in his power, to have kept his mind free from the enslaving influence of corrupt affections. Were not this the case, brute animals might be the objects of moral blame, as well as man. Some beasts are reckoned savage and cruel, others treacherous and false: we dislike, we hate creatures so ill constituted: but we do not blame nor condemn them, as we do rational agents; because they are not supposed to have a sense of right and wrong, nor freedom and power of directing their actions according to that inward rule. We must therefore admit, that the idea of freedom,

of

of a power of regulating our will and actions according to certain rules, is essential to the moral feeling. On the system of universal necessity, abstracted from this feeling, tho' certain affections and actions might excite our approbation, and others our dislike, there could be no place for blame or remorse. All the ideas would entirely vanish, which at present are suggested by the words *ought* and *should*, when applied to moral conduct.

Here then is another instance of a natural feeling, opposed to philosophic truth, analogous to what is before considered. It is the more remarkable, that it has given rise to those disputes about liberty and necessity, which have subsisted thro' all ages in the inquiring world; which, since the earliest accounts of philosophy, have run thro' all different sects of philosophers, and have been ingrafted into most of the religious systems. We are now able, I imagine, to give a clear and satisfactory account why the different

ferent parties never could agree; becaufe, in truth, the feeling of liberty, which we have, does not agree with the real fact. Thofe who were boldeft in their inquiries, traced out the philofophic truth: they faw that all things proceeded in a neceffary train of caufes and effects, which rendered it impoffible for them, to act otherways than they did; and to this fyftem they adhered, without yielding to natural feelings. Thofe again, who had not courage to oppofe the firft and moft obvious feelings of their heart, ftopped fhort, and adhered to liberty. It is obfervable, that the fide of liberty has always been the moft popular, and moft generally embraced: and, upon this fyftem, all popular difcourfes and exhortations muft needs proceed. Even thofe perfons, whofe philofophical tenets are built upon the fyftem of neceffity, find themfelves obliged to defert that fyftem, in popular argument, and to adopt the ftile and language of thofe who efpoufe liberty. Among the antients, the great affertors of neceffity were the Stoicks;

a fea severe and rigid sect, whose professed doctrine it was, to subdue all our feelings to philosophy. The Platonics, Academics and Epicureans, who embraced a softer scheme of philosophy, and were more men of the world than the Stoics, leaned to the side of liberty. Both parties have their own advantages in reasoning; and both, when pushed, run into difficulties, from which they can never extricate themselves. The advocates for liberty talk with great advantage upon the moral powers of man, and his character as an accountable being: but are at a loss, how to give any view of the universe, as a regular pre-adjusted plan; and when urged with the connection betwixt the motive and the action, and the necessary train of causes and effects, which results from admitting it to be a fixed connection, they find themselves greatly embarrassed. Here the patrons of necessity triumph. They have manifestly all the advantages of speculative argument; whilst they fail in accounting for man's moral powers, and struggle in vain to reconcile to their syftem, the teftimony which confcience clearly gives to freedom.

LET us then fairly acknowledge, concerning both thefe claffes of philofophers, that they were partly in the right, and partly in the wrong. They divided, as it were, the truth betwixt them. The one had abftract reafon on their fide: the other had natural feeling. In endeavouring to reconcile thefe oppofites, both parties failed; and the vain attempt has rendered the controverfy difficult and perplexed. After having afcertained the foundation, upon which the doctrine of neceffity is built, and which feems incapable of being fhaken, let us fairly and candidly take our nature as we find it, which will lead us to this conclufion, that tho' man, in truth, is a neceffary agent, having all his actions determined by fixed and immutable laws; yet that, this being concealed from him, he acts with the conviction of being a free agent. It is concealed from him,
I fay,

I say, as to the purposes of action: for whatever discoveries he makes as a philosopher, these affect not his conduct as a man. In principle and speculation, let him be a most rigid fatalist; he has nevertheless all the feelings which would arise from power over his own actions. He is angry at himself when he has done wrong. He praises and blames just like other men: nor can all his principles set him above the reach of self-condemnation and remorse, when conscience at any time smites him. It is true, that a man of this belief, when he is seeking to make his mind easy, after some bad action, may reason upon the principles of necessity, that, according to the constitution of his nature, it was impossible for him to have acted any other part. But this will give him little relief. In spite of all reasonings, his remorse will subsist. Nature never intended us to act upon this plan; and our natural principles are too deeply rooted, to give way to philosophy. This case is precisely similar to that of contingency. A feeling of liberty,

which

which I now fcruple not to call deceitful, is fo interwoven with our nature, that it has an equal effect in action, as if we were really endued with fuch a power.

Having explained, at full length, this remarkable feeling of liberty, and examined, as we went along, fome arguments againft neceffity that are founded upon it; we now proceed to handle this feeling, as we have done that of contingency, with regard to its final caufe. And in this branch of our nature are difplayed the greateft wifdom, and the greateft goodnefs. Man muft be fo conftituted, in order to attain the proper improvement of his nature, in virtue and happinefs. Put the cafe, he were entirely divefted of his prefent ideas of liberty: fuppofe him to fee and conceive his own nature, and the conftitution of things, in the light of ftrict philofophic truth; in the fame light they are beheld by the deity: to conceive himfelf, and all his actions, neceffarily linked into the great chain of caufes and effects, which

ren-

renders the whole order both of the natural and moral world unalterably determined in every article: fuppofe, I fay, our natural feelings, our practical ideas to fuit and tally with this, which is the real plan; and what would follow? Why, an entire derangement of our prefent fyftem of action, efpecially with regard to the motives which now lead us to virtue. There would ftill indeed be ground for the love of virtue, as the beft conftitution of nature, and the only fure foundation of happinefs; and, in this view, we might be grieved when we found ourfelves deficient in good principles. But this would be all. We could feel no inward felf-approbation on doing well, no remorfe on doing ill; becaufe both the good and the ill were neceffary and unavoidable. There would be no more place for applaufe or blame among mankind: none of that generous indignation we now feel at the bad, as perfons who have abufed and perverted their rational powers: no more notion of accountablenefs for the ufe of thofe powers: no

fenfe

sense of ill desert, or just punishment annexed to crimes as their due; nor of any reward merited by worthy and generous actions. All these ideas, and feelings, so useful to men in their moral conduct, vanish at once with the feeling of liberty. There would be field for no other passions but love and hatred, sorrow and pity: and the sense of *duty*, of being *obliged* to certain things which we *ought* to perform, must be quite extinguished; for we can have no conception of moral *obligation*, without supposing a power in the agent over his own actions.

It appears then most fit and wise, that we should be endued with a sense of liberty; without which, man must have been ill qualified for acting his present part. That artificial light, in which the feeling of liberty presents the moral world to our view, answers all the good purposes of making the actions of man entirely dependent upon himself. His happiness and misery appear to be in his own power. He appears praiseworthy

worthy or culpable, according as he improves or neglects his rational faculties. The idea of his being an accountable creature arises. Reward seems due to merit; punishment to crimes. He feels the force of moral obligation. In short, new passions arise, and a variety of new springs are set in motion, to make way for new exertions of reason and activity. In all which, tho' man is really actuated by laws of necessary influence, yet he seems to move himself: and whilst the universal system is gradually carried on to perfection by the first mover, that powerful hand, which winds up and directs the great machine, is never brought into sight.

It will now be proper to answer some objections, which may be urged against the doctrine we have advanced. One, which at first, may seem of considerable weight, is, that we found virtue altogether upon a deceitful feeling of liberty, which, it may be alledged, is neither a secure nor an honourable foundation.

dation. But, in the firſt place, I deny that we have founded it altogether upon a deceitful feeling. For, independent of the deceitful feeling of liberty, there is in the nature of man a firm foundation for virtue. He muſt be ſenſible that virtue is eſſentially preferable to vice; that it is the juſt order, the perfection and happineſs of his nature. For, ſuppoſing him only endued with the principle of ſelf-love; this principle will lead him to diſtinguiſh moral good from evil, ſo far as to give ground for loving the one, and hating the other: as he muſt needs ſee that benevolence, juſtice, temperance, and the other virtues, are the neceſſary means of his happineſs, and that all vice and wickedneſs introduce diſorder and miſery. But man is endued with a ſocial as well as a ſelfiſh principle, and has an immediate ſatisfaction and pleaſure in the happineſs of others, which is a further ground for diſtinguiſhing and loving virtue. All this, I ſay, takes place, laying aſide the deceitful feeling of liberty, and ſuppoſing all our notions to be

ad-

adjusted to the system of necessity. I add, that there is nothing in the above doctrine, to exclude the perception, of a certain beauty and excellency in virtue, according to lord *Shaftesbury* and the antient Philosophers; which may, for ought we know, render it lovely and admirable to all rational beings. It appears to us, unquestionably, under the form of intrinsick excellency, even when we think not of its tendency to our happiness. Ideas of moral obligation, of remorse, of merit, and all that is connected with this way of thinking, arise from, what may be called, a wise delusion in our nature concerning liberty: but, as this affects only a certain modification of our ideas of virtue and vice, there is nothing in it, to render the foundation of virtue, either unsecure or dishonourable. Unsecure it does not render it, because, as now observed, virtue partly stands firm upon a separate foundation, independent of these feelings; and even where built upon these feelings, it is still built upon human nature. For though these feelings of li-

berty vary from the truth of things, they are, nevertheless, essential to the nature of man. We act upon them, and cannot act otherways. And therefore, tho' the distinction betwixt virtue and vice, had no other foundation but these feelings, (which is not the case) it would still have an immoveable and secure foundation in human nature. As for the supposed dishonour done to virtue, by resting its authority, in any degree, on a deceitful feeling, there is so little ground for this part of the objection, that, on the contrary, our doctrine most highly exalts virtue. For the above described artificial sense of liberty, is wholly contrived to support virtue, and to give its dictates the force of a law. Hereby it is discovered to be, in a singular manner, the care of the Deity; and a peculiar sort of glory is thrown around it. The Author of nature, has not rested it, upon the ordinary feelings and principles of human nature, as he has rested our other affections and appetites, even those which are most necessary to our existence. But a
sort

sort of extraordinary machinery is introduced for its sake. Human nature is forced, as it were, out of its course, and made to receive a nice and artificial set of feelings; merely that conscience may have a commanding power, and virtue be set as on a throne. This could not otherways be brought about, but by means of the deceitful feeling of liberty, which therefore is a greater honour to virtue, a higher recommendation of it, than if our conceptions were, in every particular, correspondent to the truth of things.

A SECOND objection which may be urged against our system, is, that it seems to represent the Deity, as acting deceitfully by his creatures. He has given them certain ideas of contingency in events, and of liberty in their own actions, by which he has, in a manner, forced them to act upon a false hypothesis; as if he were unable, to carry on the government of this world, did his creatures conceive things, according to the real truth.

truth. This objection is, in a great measure, obviated, by what we observed in the introduction to this essay, concerning our sensible ideas. It is universally allowed by modern philosophers, that the perceptions of our external senses, are not always agreeable to strict truth, but so contrived, as rather to answer the purposes of use. Now, if it be called a deceit in our senses, not to give us just representations of the material world, the Deity must be the author of this deceit, as much as he is, of that which prevails in our moral ideas. But no just objection can ly against the conduct of the Deity, in either case. Our senses, both internal and external, are given us for different ends and purposes; some to discover truth, others to make us happy and virtuous. The senses which are appropriated to the discovery of truth, unerringly answer their end. So do the senses, which are appropriated to virtue and happiness. And, in this view, it is no material objection, that the same sense does not answer both ends. As to the other part of
the

the objection, that it must imply imperfection in the Deity, if he cannot establish virtue but upon a delusive foundation; we may be satisfied how fallacious this reasoning is, by reflecting upon the numberless appearances, of moral evil and disorder in this world. From these appearances, much more strongly, were there any force in this reasoning, might we infer imperfection in the Deity; seeing the state of this world, in many particulars, does not answer the notions we are apt to form, of supreme power conducted by perfect wisdom and goodness. But, in truth, there is nothing in our doctrine, which can justly argue imperfection in the Deity. For it is abundantly plain, first, that it is a more perfect state of things, and more worthy of the Deity, to have all events going on with unbroken order, in a fixed train of causes and effects; than to have every thing desultory and contingent. And, if such a being as man, was to be placed in this world, to act his present part; it was necessary, that he should have a notion of contingency in events,

vents, and of liberty in his own actions. The objection therefore, on the whole, amounts to no more, than that the Deity cannot work contradictions. For, if it was fit and wise, that man should think and act, as a free agent, it was impossible this could be otherways accomplished, than by endowing him with a sense of liberty: and if it was also fit and wise, that universal necessity should be the real plan of the universe, this sense of liberty could be no other than a deceitful one.

Another objection may perhaps be raised against us in this form. If it was necessary for man to be constituted, with such an artificial feeling, why was he endowed with so much knowledge, as to unravel the mystery? What purpose does it serve, to let in just so much light, as to discover the disguised appearance of the moral world, when it was intended, that his conduct should be adjusted to this disguised appearance? To this, I answer, first, that the discovery, when made, cannot possibly be of any bad consequence;
and

and next, that a good confequence, of very great importance, refults from it. No bad confequence, I fay, enfues from the difcovery, that liberty and contingency are deceitful feelings; for the cafe is confeffedly parallel in the natural world, where no harm has enfued. After we have difcovered, by philofophy, that feveral of the appearances of nature, are only ufeful illufions, that fecondary qualities exift not in matter, and that our fenfible ideas, in various inftances, do not correfpond to philofophic truth; after thefe difcoveries are made, do they, in the leaft, affect even the philofopher himfelf in ordinary action? Does not he, in common with the reft of mankind, proceed, as it is fit he fhould, upon the common fyftem of appearances and natural feelings? As little, in the prefent cafe, do our fpeculations about liberty and neceffity, counteract the plan of nature. Upon the fyftem of liberty we do, and muft act: and no difcoveries, made concerning the illufive nature of that feeling, are

capable

capable of difappointing, in any degree, the intention of the Deity.

But this is not all. Thefe difcoveries are alfo of excellent ufe, as they furnifh us with one of the ftrongeft arguments, for the exiftence of the Deity, and as they fet the wifdom and goodnefs of his providence, in the moft ftriking light. Nothing carries in it more exprefs chara&ters of defign; nothing can be conceived more oppofite to chance, than a plan fo artfully contrived, for adjufting our impreffions and feelings to the purpofes of life. For here things are carried off, as it were, from the ftraight line; taken out of the courfe, in which they would of themfelves proceed; and fo moulded, as forcibly, and againft their nature, to be fubfervient to man. His mind does not receive the impreffion of the moral world, in the fame manner, as wax receives the impreffion of a feal. It does not refle&t the image of it, in the fame manner, as a mirror refle&ts its images: it has a peculiar caft and turn given to its
con-

conceptions, admirably ordered to exalt virtue, to the higheſt pitch. Theſe conceptions are indeed illuſive, yet, which is wonderful, it is by this very circumſtance, that, in man, two of the moſt oppoſite things in nature, are happily reconciled, liberty and neceſſity; having this illuſtrious effect, that in him are accumulated, all the prerogatives both of a neceſſary and free agent. The diſcovery of ſuch a marvelous adjuſtment, which is more directly oppoſed to chance, than any other thing conceiveable, muſt neceſſarily give us the ſtrongeſt impreſſion of a wiſe deſigning cauſe. And now a ſufficient reaſon appears, for ſuffering man to make this ſurpriſing diſcovery. The Almighty has let us ſo far into his councils, as to afford the juſteſt foundation, for admiring and adoring his wiſdom. It is a remark worthy to be made, that the capacities of man ſeem, in general, to have a tendency beyond the wants and occaſions of his preſent ſtate. This has been often obſerved with reſpect to his wiſhes and deſires. The ſame holds as to his intellectual faculties, which, sometimes, as in the instance before us, run beyond the limits of what is strictly necessary for him to know, in his present circumstances, and let in upon him some glimmerings of higher and nobler discoveries. A veil is thrown over nature, where it is not useful for him to behold it. And yet, sometimes, by turning aside that veil a very little, he is admitted to a fuller view; that his admiration of nature, and the God of nature, may be increased; that his curiosity and love of truth may be fed; and, perhaps, that some *augurium*, some intimation, may be given, of his being designed for a future, more exalted period of being; when attaining the full maturity of his nature, he shall no longer stand in need of artificial impressions, but shall feel and act according to the strictest truth of things.

ESSAYS

ESSAYS

UPON THE

PRINCIPLES of MORALITY

AND

NATURAL RELIGION.

PART II.

ESSAY I.

Of BELIEF.

BELIEF is a term so familiar, as to have escaped the inquiry of all philosophers, except the author of the treatise of human nature. And yet the subject is, by no means, so plain as to admit of no doubts nor difficulties. This author has made two propositions sufficiently evident; first, that belief is not any separate action or perception of the mind, but a modification of our perceptions, or a certain manner of conceiving propositions. 2d, That it does not accompany every one of our perceptions. A man, in some circumstances, sees objects double, but he does not believe them to be double. He can form the idea of a golden mountain: he can form the idea of it, as of a certain size, and as existing in a certain place: but he does not believe it to be existing.

HAVING proved that belief is not a separate perception, but only a modification

of

of some perceptions, our author goes on to explain the nature of this modification. And his doctrine is, that belief making no alteration upon the idea, as to its parts and composition, must consist in the lively manner of conceiving the idea; and that, in reality, a lively idea and belief are the same. I have a high opinion of this author's acuteness and penetration; but no authority can prevail with me to embrace such a doctrine. For, at this rate, credulity and a lively imagination would be always connected, which does not hold in fact. Poetry and painting produce lively ideas, but they seldom produce belief. For my part, I have no difficulty to form as lively a conception of Cesar's dying in his bed, descanting upon the vanity of ambition, or dictating rules of government to his successor, as of his being put to death in the senate-house. Nothing is told with more vivacity, than the death of Cyrus, in a pitched battle with the queen of the Scythians, who dipped his head, as we are told, in a vessel full of blood, saying, " Satiate thyself
" with

OF BELIEF. 223

" with blood, of which thou waſt ever thir-
" ſty." Yet, upon comparing circumſtances and authors, the more probable opinion
is, that Cyrus died in his bed.

It may be obſerved, at the ſame time, that
the concluſion is very lame, which this author
draws from his premiſes. Belief makes no
alteration upon the idea, as to its parts and
compoſition. It can only therefore conſiſt
in a modification of the idea. But does it
follow, that it conſiſts in a lively concepti-
tion of the idea, which is but one of many
modifications? There is not here the ſha-
dow of an inference.

Our author indeed urges, that true hiſtory takes faſt hold of the mind, and preſents
its objects in a more lively manner, than any
fabulous narration can do. Every man muſt
judge for himſelf: I cannot admit this to
be my caſe. Hiſtory, no doubt, takes faſt-
er hold of the mind, than any fiction told
in the plain hiſtorical ſtile. But can any
man

man doubt, who has not an hypothesis to defend, that poetry makes a stronger impression than history? Let a man, if he has feelings, attend the celebrated Garrick in the character of Richard, or in that of king Lear; and he will find, that dramatic representations make strong and lively impressions, which history seldom comes up to.

But now, if it shall be supposed, that history presents its objects in a more lively manner, than can be done by dramatic or epic poetry; it will not therefore follow, that a lively idea is the same with belief. I read a passage in Virgil. Let it be the episode of Nisus and Euryalus. I read a passage in Livy, *sciz.* the sacking of Rome by the Gauls. If I have a more lively idea of the latter story, I put it to my author, to point out the cause of this effect. He surely will not affirm, that it is the force of expression, or harmony of numbers: for, in these particulars, the historian cannot be compared to the poet. It is evident, that no other satisfactory

OF BELIEF.

factory account of the matter can be given, but this, that Livy's superior influence upon the imagination, is the effect of his being considered, as a true historian. The most, then, that our author can make of his observation, supposing it to hold true in fact, is, that the authority of the historian produces belief, and that belief produces a more lively idea, than any fabulous narration can do. The truth of the matter is, that belief and a lively conception, are really two distinct modifications of the idea; which, tho' often conjoined, are not only separable in the imagination, but in fact are often separated. Truth, indeed, bestows a certain degree of vivacity upon our ideas. At the same time, I cannot admit, that history exceeds dramatic or epic poetry, in conveying a lively conception of facts; because it appears evident, that, in works of imagination, the want of truth, is more than compensated by sentiment and language.

F f   SOME-

Sometimes, indeed, belief is the result of a lively impression. A dramatic representation is one instance, when it affects us so much, as to draw off the attention from every other object, and even from ourselves. In this situation, we don't consider the actor, but conceive him to be the very man whose character he assumes. We have that very man before our eyes. We perceive him as existing and acting, and believe him to be existing and acting. This belief, however, is but momentary. It vanishes, like a dream, so soon as we are rouzed by any trivial circumstance, to a consciousness of ourselves, and of the place we are in. Nor is the lively impression, even in this case, the cause of belief, but only the occasion of it, by diverting the attention of the mind, from itself and its situation. It is in some such manner, that the idea of a spectre in the dark, which fills the mind, and diverts it from itself, is, by the force of imagination, converted into a reality. We think we see

and

and hear it. We are convinced of it, and believe the matter to be so.

Rejecting therefore this author's opinion, the real truth appears to be this. There is a certain peculiar manner of perceiving objects, and conceiving propositions, which, being a simple feeling, cannot be described, but is expressed by the word belief. The causes of this modification, termed belief, are the authority of my own senses, and the authority of others, who either relate facts upon the authority of their senses, or what they have heard at second or third hand. So that belief, mediately or immediately, is founded upon the authority of our senses. We are so constituted by nature, as to put trust in our senses. Nor, in general, is it in our power to disbelieve our senses: they have authority with us irresistible. There is but one exception that I can think of. Finding, by experience, that we have been sometimes led into an error, by trusting some particular perceptions, the remembrance

brance of these instances, counter-balances the authority of our perception in the like cases, and either keeps the mind suspended, or, perhaps, makes it rest in a conviction, that the perception is erroneous.

With regard to the evidence of my own senses, tho' I cannot admit, that the essence of belief consists in the vivacity of the impression, I so far agree with our author, that vivacity and belief, in this case, are always conjoined. A mountain I have once seen, I believe to be existing, tho' I am a thousand miles from it; and the image or idea I have of that mountain, is more lively and more distinct, than of any I can form merely by the force of imagination. But this is far from being the case, as above observed, of ideas raised in my mind by the force of language,

Belief arising from the evidence of others, rests upon a different foundation. Veracity and a disposition to believe, are correspond-

OF BELIEF.

sponding principles in the nature of man; and, in the main, these principles are so adjusted, that men are not often deceived. The disposition we have to believe, is qualified by the opinion we have of the witness, and the nature of the story he relates. But, supposing a concurrence of all other circumstances to prompt our belief, yet, if the speaker pretends only to amuse, without confining himself to truth, his narration will not, in the smallest degree, prompt our belief; let him enliven it with the strongest colours that poetry is master of.

I have only to add, that tho' our own senses, and the testimony of others, are the proper causes of belief; yet that these causes are more or less efficacious, according to the temper of mind we are in at the time. Hope and fear are influenced by passion, so is belief. Hope and fear are modifications of our conception of future events. If the event be agreeable, and the probability of its existence, be great, our conception of its existence takes on a modification, which is called hope. If the event be extremely agreeable, and the probability of its exifting do greatly preponderate, our hope is increafed proportionally, and fometimes is converted into a firm belief, that it will really happen. Upon weak minds, the delightfulnefs of the expected event, will of itfelf have that effect. The imagination, fired with the profpect, augments the probability, 'till it convert it to a firm perfuafion or belief. On the other hand, if fear get the afcendent, by a conceived improbability of the exiftence of the event, the mind defponds, and fear is converted into a firm belief, that the event will not happen. The operations of the mind are quite fimilar, where the event in view is difagreeable.

ESSAY

ESSAY II.

Of the IDEA *of* SELF *and of* PERSONAL IDENTITY.

HAD we no original impressions but those of the external senses, according to the author of the treatise of human nature, we never could have any consciousness of *self*; because such consciousness cannot arise from any external sense. Mankind would be in a perpetual reverie; ideas would be constantly floating in the mind; and no man be able to connect his ideas with *himself.* Neither could there be any idea of *personal identity.* For a man, cannot consider himself to be the same person, in different circumstances, when he has no idea or consciousness of *himself* at all.

BEINGS there may be, who are thus constituted: but man is none of these beings. It is an undoubted truth, that he has an original feeling, or consciousness of himself,
and

and of his exiſtence; which, for the moſt part, accompanies every one of his impreſſions and ideas, and every action of his mind and body. I ſay, for the moſt part; for the faculty or internal ſenſe, which is the cauſe of this peculiar perception, is not always in action. In a dead ſleep, we have no conſciouſneſs of ſelf. We dream ſometimes without this conſciouſneſs: and even ſome of our waking hours paſs without it. A reverie is nothing elſe, but a wandering of the mind through its ideas, without carrying along the perception of ſelf.

This conſciouſneſs or perception of ſelf, is, at the ſame time, of the livelieſt kind. Self-preſervation is every one's peculiar duty; and the vivacity of this perception, is neceſſary to make us attentive to our own intereſt, and, particularly, to ſhun every appearance of danger. When a man is in a reverie, he has no circumſpection, nor any manner of attention to his own intereſt.

PERSONAL IDENTITY.

'Tis remarkable, that one has scarce any chance to fall asleep, 'till this perception vanish. Its vivacity keeps the mind in a certain degree of agitation, which bars sleep. A fall of water disposes to sleep. It fixes the attention, both by sound and sight, and, without creating much agitation, occupies the mind, so as to make it forget itself. Reading of some books has the same effect.

It is this perception, or consciousness of self, carried through all the different stages of life, and all the variety of action, which is the foundation of *personal identity*. It is, by means of this perception, that I consider myself to be the same person, in all varieties of fortune, and every change of circumstance.

The main purpose of this short essay, is to introduce an observation, that it is not by any argument or reasoning, I conclude myself to be the same person, I was ten years ago. This conclusion rests entirely upon the feeling of identity, which accompanies me through all my changes, and which is the only connecting principle, that binds together, all the various thoughts and actions of my life. Far less is it by any argument, or chain of reasoning, that I discover my own existence. It would be strange indeed, if every man's existence was kept a secret from him, 'till the celebrated argument was invented, that *cogito ergo sum*. And if a fact, that, to common understanding, appears self-evident, is not to be relied on without an argument; why should I take for granted, without an argument, that I think, more than that I exist? For surely I am not more conscious of thinking, than of existing.

Upon this subject, I shall just suggest a thought, which will be more fully insisted on afterwards; that any doctrine, which leads to a distrust of our senses, must land in universal scepticism. If natural feelings, whether from internal or external senses, are not admitted as evidence of truth, I cannot

not see, that we can be certain of any fact whatever. It is clear, from what is now observed, that, upon this sceptical system, we cannot be certain even of our own existence *.

* The deceitful feeling of liberty, unfolded in the essay upon liberty and necessity, may perhaps embarrass some readers, as in some measure contradictory to the position here laid down. But the matter is easily cleared. Natural feelings are satisfying evidence of truth; and, in fact, have full authority over us, unless in some singular cases, where we are admonished by counter-feelings, or by reasoning, not to give implicit trust. This is a sufficient foundation for all the arguments, that are built upon the authority of our senses, in point of evidence. The feeling of liberty is a very singular case. The reasons are clearly traced for the necessity of this delusive feeling, which distinguishes it in a very particular manner, and leaves no room, to draw any consequence from it, to our other feelings. But there is, besides, a circumstance yet more distinguishing, in this delusive feeling of liberty, which entirely exempts it, from being an exception to the general rule above laid down. It is this ; that the feeling is by no means entire on the side of liberty. It is counter-balanced by other feelings, which, in many instances, afford such a conviction of the necessary influence of motives, that physical and moral necessity can scarce be distinguished. The sense of liberty operates chiefly in the after reflection. But, previous to the action, there is no distinct or clear feeling, that it can happen otherways, than in connection with its proper motive. Here the feelings being, on the whole, opposite to each other, nothing

can be inferred from this case, to derogate from the evidence of feelings that are clear, cogent and authoritative; and to which, nothing can be opposed, from the side of reason or counter-feelings. So that our principle remains safe and unshaken, that a general distrust of our senses, internal or external, must land us in universal scepticism.

ESSAY

ESSAY III.

Of the Authority *of our* Senses.

IN a former essay are pointed out some instances, in which our senses may be called deceitful*. They are of two sorts. One is, when the deception is occasioned by indisposition of the organ, remoteness of place, grossness of the medium, or the like; which distort the appearances of objects, and make them be seen double, or greater or less, than they really are. In such instances, the perception is always faint, obscure or confused: and they noway invalidate the authority of the senses, in general, when, abstracting from such accidental obstructions, the perception is lively, strong and distinct. In the other sort, there is a deception established by the laws of nature; as in the case of secondary qualities, taken notice of in that essay; whence it was inferred, that nature does not always give us such correct perceptions, as correspond to the philosophic truth

* Essay upon liberty and necessity.

truth of things. Notwithstanding of which, the testimony of our senses still remains, as a sufficient ground of confidence and trust. For, in all these cases, where there is this sort of established deception, nature furnishes means for coming at the truth. As in this very instance of secondary qualities, philosophy easily corrects the false appearances, and teaches us, that they are rather to be considered, as impressions made upon the mind, than as qualities of the object. A remedy being thus provided to the deception, our belief, so far as it can be influenced by reason, is the more confirmed, with regard to our other sensations, where there is no appearance of illusion. But this is not the whole of the matter. When any sense presents to our view, an appearance that may be called deceitful, we plainly discover some useful purpose intended. The deceit is not the effect of an imperfect or arbitrary constitution; but wisely contrived, to give us such notice of things, as may best suit the purposes of life. From this very consideration, we are the more confirm-

ed

ed in the veracity of nature. Particular inſtances, in which, our ſenſes are accommodated to the uſes of life, rather than to the ſtrictneſs of truth, are rational exceptions, which ſerve, the more firmly, to eſtabliſh the general rule. And, indeed, when we have nothing but our ſenſes to direct our conduct, with regard to external objects, it would be ſtrange, if there ſhould be any juſt ground, for a general diſtruſt of them. But there is no ſuch thing. There is nothing to which all mankind are more neceſſarily determined, than to put confidence in their ſenſes. We entertain no doubt of their authority, becauſe we are ſo conſtituted, that it is not in our power to doubt.

When the authority of our ſenſes is thus founded on the neceſſity of our nature, and confirmed by conſtant experience, it cannot but appear ſtrange, that it ſhould come into the thought of any man to call it in queſtion. But the influence of novelty is great; and when a bold genius, in ſpite of common ſenſe,

sense, and common feelings, will strike out new paths to himself, 'tis not easy to foresee, how far his airy metaphysical notions may carry him. A late author, who gives us a treatise concerning the principles of human knowledge, by denying the reality of external objects, strikes at the root of the authority of our senses, and thereby paves the way to the most inveterate scepticism. For what reliance can we have upon our senses, if they deceive us in a point so material? If we can be prevailed upon, to doubt of the reality of external objects, the next step will be, to doubt of what passes in our own minds, of the reality of our ideas and perceptions. For we have not a stronger consciousness, nor a clearer conviction of the one, than of the other. And the last step will be, to doubt of our own existence; for it is shown in the essay immediately foregoing, that we have no certainty of this fact, but what depends upon sense and feeling.

It

It is reported, that doctor Berkeley, the author of the abovementioned treatise, was moved to adopt this whimsical opinion, to get free of some arguments, urged by materialists against the existence of the Deity. If so, he has been unhappy in his experiment; for this doctrine, if it should not lead to universal scepticism, affords, at least, a shrewd argument in favours of Atheism. If I can only be conscious of what passes in my own mind, and if I cannot trust my senses, when they give me notice of external and independent existences; it follows, that I am the only being in the world; at least, that I can have no evidence from my senses, of any other being, body or spirit. This is certainly an unwary concession; because it deprives us of our principal, or only, inlet to the knowledge of the Deity. Laying aside sense and feeling, this learned divine will find it a difficult task, to point out by what other means it is, that we make the discovery of the above important truth. But of this more afterwards.

Were there nothing else in view, but to eftablifh the reality of external objects, it would be fcarce worth while, to beftow much thought, in folving metaphyfical paradoxes againft their exiftence, which are better confuted by common fenfe and experience. But, as the above doctrine appears to have very extenfive confequences, and to ftrike at the root of the moft valuable branches of human knowledge; an attempt to re-eftablifh the authority of our fenfes, by detecting the fallacy of the arguments that have been urged againft it, may, it is hoped, not be unacceptable to the public. The attempt, at any rate, is neceffary in this work, the main purpofe of which is, to fhow that our fenfes, external and internal, are the true fources, from whence the knowledge of the Deity is derived to us.

In order to afford fatisfaction upon a fubject, which is eafier felt than expreft, it will be proper, to give a diftinct analyfis of the operations of thofe fenfes, by which we perceive

ceive external objects. And, if this be once clearly apprehended, it will not be a matter of difficulty, to anfwer the feveral objections, which have been urged againſt their exiſtence.

The impreſſions of the external ſenſes are of different kinds. Some we have at the organs of ſenſe, ſuch as ſmelling, taſting, touching. Some are made upon us as from a diſtance, ſuch as hearing and ſeeing. From the ſenſe of feeling, are derived the impreſſions of body, ſolidity and external exiſtence. Laying my hand upon this table, I perceive a thing ſmooth and hard, preſſing upon my hand, and which is perceived as more diſtant from me, than my hand is. From the ſight, we have the impreſſions of motion and of colour; and from the ſight as well as from the touch, thoſe of extenſion and figure. But it is more material to obſerve, upon the preſent ſubject, that from ſight as well as touch, we have the impreſſion of things
as

as having an independent and continued or permanent exiſtence.

Let us endeavour to explain this modification of independency and permanent exiſtence of the objects of ſight and touch, for it is a cardinal point. To begin with the objects of ſight. I caſt my eye upon a tree, and perceive colour, figure, extention, and ſometimes motion. If this be a complete analyſis of the perception, ſubſtance is not diſcoverable by ſight. But upon attentively examining this perception, to try if there be any thing more in it, I find one circumſtance omitted, that the above particulars, are not perceived as ſo many ſeparate exiſtences, having no relation to each other, but as cloſely united and connected. When looking around on different objects, I perceive colour in one quarter, motion in a ſecond, and extenſion in a third; the appearance theſe make in my mind, are in nothing ſimilar to the impreſſion made by a tree, where the extenſion, motion, and other qualities, are
introduced

introduced into the mind, under the modification of an intimate connection and union. But in what manner are they united and connected? Of this, every person can give an account, that they are perceived as inhering in, or belonging to some *substance* or *thing*, of which they are *qualities*; and that, by their reference to this substance or thing, they are thus closely united and connected. Thus it is, that the impression of *substance*, as well as of *qualities*, is derived from sight. And it is also to be attended to, as a part of the total impression, that as the qualities appear to belong to their substance, and to inhere in it, so both the substance and its qualities, which we call the tree, are perceived as altogether independent of us, as really existing, and as having a permanent existence.

A similar impression is made upon us, by means of the sense of feeling. It is observed above, that, from the touch, we have the impressions, of body, solidity and external

nal exiftence; and we have, from the fame fenfe, the impreffions of foftnefs and hardnefs, fmoothnefs and roughnefs. Now, when I lay my hand upon this table, I have an impreffion, not only of fmoothnefs, hardnefs, figure and extenfion, but alfo of a thing I call *body*, of which the above are perceived as *qualities*. Smoothnefs, hardnefs, extenfion and figure are felt, not as feparate and unconnected exiftences, but as inhering in and belonging to fomething I call *body*, which is really exifting, and which has an independent and permanent exiftence. And it is this body, with its feveral qualities, which I exprefs by the word *table*.

The above analyfis of the impreffions of fight and touch, will be beft illuftrated, by a comparifon with the impreffions made by the other fenfes. I hear a found, or I feel a fmell. Attending to thefe impreffions, I perceive nothing but found or fmell. They are not perceived as the qualities or properties of any body, thing or fubftance.

They

They make their appearance in the mind as simple existences; and there is no impression made of independency, or permanent existence. Did seeing and feeling carry us no further, we never could have the least conception of substance.

'Tis not a little surprising, that philosophers, who discourse so currently of *qualities*, should affect so much doubt and hesitation about *substance*; seeing these are relative ideas, and imply each other. For what other reason do we call figure a quality, but that we perceive it, not as a separate existence, but as belonging to something that is figured; and which thing we call *substance*, because it is not a property of any other thing, but is a thing which subsists by itself, or has an independent existence. Did we perceive figure, as we perceive sound, it would not be considered as a quality. In a word, a quality is not intelligible, unless upon supposition of some other thing, of which it is the quality. Sounds indeed, and smells are also

con-

considered as qualities. But this proceeds from habit, not from original perception. For, having once acquired the distinction betwixt a *thing* and its *qualities*, and finding sound and smell, more to resemble *qualities* than *substances*, we readily come into the use of considering them as qualities.

Another thing is to be observed with regard to those things, which are perceived as qualities by the sight and touch; that we cannot form a conception of them, independent of the beings to which they belong. It is not in our power, to separate, even in imagination, colour, figure, motion and extension from body or substance. There is no such thing as conceiving motion by itself, abstracted from some body which is in motion. Let us try ever so often, our attempts will be in vain, to form an idea of a triangle independent of a body which has that figure. We cannot conceive a body that is not figured; and we can as little conceive a figure without a body; for this would be to conceive

ceive a figure, as having a separate existence, at the same time, that we conceive it, as having no separate existence; or to conceive it, at once, to be a quality, and not a quality. Thus it comes out, that *substance*, as well as *quality*, makes a part, not only of every perception of sight and touch, but of every conception we can form, of colour, figure, extension and motion. Taking in the whole train of our ideas, there is not one more familiar to us, than that of *substance*, a being or thing which has qualities.

When these things are considered, I cannot readily discover, by what wrong conception of the matter, Mr. *Locke* has been led, to talk so obscurely and indistinctly of the idea of substance. 'Tis no wonder, he should be difficulted, to form an idea of substance in general, abstracted from all properties, when such abstraction is altogether beyond the reach of our conception. But there is nothing more easy, than to form an idea of any particular substance with its properties.

perties. Yet this has some how escaped him. When he forms the idea of a horse or a stone, he admits nothing into the idea, but a collection of several simple ideas of sensible qualities †. " And because, says he, we " cannot conceive how these qualities should " subsist alone, nor one in another, we sup- " pose them existing in, and supported by " some common subject; which support, we " denote by the name *substance*, tho' it be " certain, we have no clear or distinct idea " of that thing we suppose a support." A single question would have unfolded the whole mystery. How comes it, that we cannot conceive qualities to subsist alone, nor one in another? Mr. *Locke* himself must have given the following answer, that the thing is not conceiveable; because a property or quality cannot subsist without the thing to which it belongs; for, if it did, that it would cease to be a property or quality. Why then does he make so faint an inference, as that we suppose qualities existing in, and supported by some common subject? It is

† Book 2d, chap. 23.

is not a bare suppofition: it is an effential part of the idea: it is neceffarily fuggefted to us by fight and touch. He obferves that we have no clear nor diftinct idea of fubftance. If he means, that we have no clear nor diftinct idea of fubftance abftracted from its properties, the thing is fo true, that we can form no idea of fubftance at all, abftracted from its properties. But it is alfo true, that we can form no idea of properties, abftracted from a fubftance. The ideas both of fubftance and of quality are perfectly in the fame condition, in this refpect; which,'tis furprifing, philofophers fhould fo little attend to. At the fame time, we have clear and diftinct ideas, of many things as they exift; tho' perhaps we have not a complete idea of any one thing. We have fuch ideas of things, as ferve to all the ufeful purpofes of life. 'Tis true, our fenfes don't reach beyond the external properties of beings. We have no direct perception of the effence and internal properties of any thing. Thefe we difcover from the effects produced. But had we fenfes directly to perceive the effence and

internal

internal properties of things, our idea of them would indeed be more full and complete, but not more clear and diſtinct, than at preſent. For, even upon that ſuppoſition, we could form no notion of ſubſtance, but by its properties internal and external. To form an idea of a thing abſtracted from all its properties, is impoſſible.

The following is the ſum of what is above laid down. By ſight and touch, we have the impreſſions of ſubſtance and body, as well as of qualities. It is not figure, extenſion, motion, that we perceive; but a thing figured, extended and moving. As we cannot form an idea of ſubſtance abſtracted from qualities, ſo we cannot form an idea of qualities abſtracted from ſubſtance. They are relative ideas, and imply each other. This is one point gained. Another is, that the idea of ſubſtance or body, thus attained, comprehends in it, independent and permanent exiſtence; that is, ſomething which exiſts independent of our perceptions, and remains the ſame, whether we perceive it or not.

In this manner are we made sensible of the real existence of things without us. The feeling is so strong, and the conviction which makes a part of the feeling, that sceptical arguments, however cunningly devised, may puzzle, but can never get the better: for such is our constitution, that we can entertain no doubt of the authority of our senses, in this particular. At the same time, every sort of experience confirms the truth of our perceptions. I see a tree at a distance, of a certain shape and size. Walking forward, I find it in its place, by the resistance it makes to my body; and, so far as I can discover by touch, it is of the same shape and size, which my eye represents it to be. I return day after day, year after year, and find the same object, with no other variation, but what the seasons and time produce. The tree is at last cut down. It is no longer to be seen or felt.

To overthrow the authority of our senses, a few particular instances, in which they

appear

appear fallacious, are of no weight. And to confirm this branch of the argument, we need but compare the evidence of our senses, with the evidence of human testimony. The comparison cannot fail to afford satisfaction. Veracity, and a disposition to rely upon human evidence, are corresponding principles, which greatly promote society. Among individuals, these principles are found to be of different degrees of strength. But, in the main, they are so proportioned to each other, that men are not often deceived. In this case, it would be but a bad argument, that we ought not to give credit to any man's testimony, because some men are defective in the principle of veracity. The only effect such instances have, or ought to have, is to correct our propensity to believe, and to bring on a habit of suspending our belief, 'till circumstances be examined. The evidence of our senses, rises undoubtedly much higher, than the evidence of human testimony. And if we continue to put trust in the latter, after many instances of being deceived, ed, we have better reason to put trust in the former, were the instances of being deceived equally numerous; which is plainly not the fact. When people are in sound health of mind and body, they are very seldom mis-led by their senses.

If I have been so lucky, as to put this subject in its proper light, it will not be a difficult task to clear it of any doubts which may arise, upon perusing the above mentioned treatise. The author boldly denies the existence of matter, and the reality of the objects of sense; contending, that there is nothing really existing without the mind of an intelligent being; in a word, reducing all to be a world of ideas. " It is an " opinion strangely prevailing among men, " (says he) that houses, mountains, rivers, " and, in a word, all sensible objects, have an " existence, natural or real, distinct from " their being perceived by the understand- " ing." He ventures to call this a manifest contradiction; and his argument against the

reality

reality of these objects, is in the following words. "The forementioned objects are things perceived by sense. We cannot perceive any thing, but our own ideas or perceptions; therefore, what we call men, houses, mountains, &c. can be nothing else but ideas or perceptions." This argument shall be examined afterwards, with the respect that is due to its author. It shall only be taken notice of by the way, that, supposing mankind to be under so strange and unaccountable a delusion, as to mistake their ideas for men, houses, mountains, &c. it will not follow, that there is in this, any manifest contradiction, or any contradiction at all. For deception is a very different thing from contradiction. But he falls from this high pretension, in the after part of his work, to argue more consistently, "that, supposing solid, figured, and moveable substances, to exist without the mind, yet we could never come to the knowledge of this *." Which is true, if our senses bear

* Sect. 18.

bear no testimony of the fact. And he adds *, " that, supposing no bodies to exist " without the mind, we might have the ve-" ry same reasons for supposing the existence " of external bodies, that we have now:" which may be true, supposing only our senses to be fallacious.

THE doctor's fundamental proposition is, that we can perceive nothing but our own ideas or perceptions. This, at best, is an ambiguous expression. For, taking perception or sensation in its proper sense, as signifying every object we perceive, it is a mere identical proposition, *sciz.* that we perceive nothing but what we perceive. But, taking the doctor's proposition as he intended it, that we can have no perception or consciousness of any thing, but what exists in our own minds, he had certainly no reason to take this assertion for granted; and yet he has never once attempted a proof of it: tho', in so bold an undertaking, as that of annihilat-

* Sect. 20.

ing the whole univerſe, his own mind excepted, he had no reaſon to hope, that an aſſertion, ſo ſingular, and ſo contradictory to common ſenſe and feeling, would be taken upon his word. It may be true, that it is not eaſy to explain, nor even to comprehend, by what means we perceive external objects. But our ignorance is, in moſt caſes, a very indifferent argument againſt matter of fact. At this rate, he may take upon him equally to deny the bulk of the operations in the natural world, which have not hitherto been explained by him, or others. And at, bottom, 'tis perhaps as difficult to explain the manner of perceiving our own ideas, or the impreſſions made upon us, as to explain the manner of perceiving external objects. The doctor, beſides, ought to have conſidered, that by this bold doctrine, he, in effect, ſets bounds to the power of nature, or of the Author of nature. If it was in the power of the Almighty, to beſtow upon man, a faculty of perceiving external objects, he has certainly done it. For, ſuppoſing the exiſtence

of

of external objects, we have no conception, how they could be otherways manifested to us, than in fact they are. Therefore, the doctor was in the right to assert, that a faculty in man to perceive external objects, would be a contradiction, and consequently a privilege not in the power of the Deity to bestow upon him. He perceived the necessity of carrying his argument so far; at the same time, sensible that this was not to be made out, he never once attempts to point at any thing like a contradiction. And if he cannot prove it to be a contradiction, the question is at an end; for, supposing only the fact to be possible, we have the very highest evidence of its reality, that our nature is capable of, no less than the testimony of our senses.

It has been urged in support of the above doctrine, that nothing is present to the mind, but the impressions made upon it, and that it cannot be conscious of any thing but what is present. This difficulty is easily solved.
For

For the propofition, that we cannot be confcious of any thing but what is prefent to the mind, or paffes within it, is taken for granted, as if it were felf-evident. And yet the direct contrary is an evident fact, *fciz.* that we are confcious of many things which are not prefent to the mind; that is, which are not, like impreffions and ideas, within the mind. Nor is there any manner of difficulty to conceive, that an impreffion may be made upon us, by an external object, in fuch a manner, as to raife a direct perception of the external object itfelf. When we attend to the operations of the external fenfes, the impreffions made upon us by external objects, are difcovered to have very different effects. In fome inftances we feel the impreffion, and are confcious of it, as an impreffion. In others, being quite unconfcious of the impreffion, we perceive only the external object. And to give full fatisfaction to the reader, upon the prefent fubject, it may perhaps not be fruitlefs, briefly to run over the operations of the feveral external

nal

nal senses, by which the mind is made conscious of external objects, and of their properties.

And first, with regard to the sense of smelling, which gives us no notice of external existences. Here the operation is of the simplest kind. It is no more but an impression made at the organ, which is perceived as an impression. Experience, 'tis true, and habit, lead us to ascribe this particular impression to some external thing as its cause. Thus, when a particular impression is made upon us, termed the sweet smell of a rose, we learn to ascribe it to a rose, tho' there is no such object within view, because that peculiar impression upon the organ of smelling, is always found to accompany the sight and touch of the body, called a rose. But that this connection is the child of experience only, will be evident from the following considerations; that, when a new smell is perceived, we are utterly at a loss, what cause to ascribe it to; and, that when a child feels a smell, it is not led to assign it

to

to any cause whatever. In this case, there can be no other difficulty, but to comprehend, in what manner the mind becomes conscious of an impression, made upon the body. Upon which, it seems sufficient to observe, that we are kept entirely ignorant, in what manner the soul and body are connected; which is no singular case. But, from our ignorance of the manner of this connection, to deny the reality of external existences, reducing all to a world of ideas, is in reality not less whimsical, than if one, after admitting the reality of external existences, should go about to deny, that we have any perception of them; merely because we cannot fully account for the manner of this perception, nor how a material substance can communicate itself to the mind, which is spirit and not matter. The same observations may be applied to the sense of hearing; with this difference only, that a sound is not perceived, at least not originally, as an impression made at the organ, but merely as an existence in the mind.

I<small>N</small>

In the senses of tasting and touching, we are conscious not only of an impression made at the organ, but also of a body which makes the impression. When I lay my hand upon this table, the impression is of a hard smooth body, which resists the motion of my hand. In this impression, there is nothing to create the least suspicion of fallacy. The body acts where it is, and it acts merely by resistance. There occurs not, therefore, any other difficulty in this case, than that mentioned above, *viz.* after what manner an impression made at an organ of the body, is communicated to, or perceived by the mind. We shall only add upon this head, that touch alone, which is the least intricate of all our feelings, is sufficient to overthrow the doctor's whole pompous system. We have, from that sense, the fullest and clearest perception of external existences, that can be conceived, subject to no doubt, ambiguity, nor even cavil. And this perception, must, at the same time, support

the

the authority of our senses, when they give us notice of external existences.

What remains to be examined, is the sense of seeing, which, 'tis presumed, the doctor had principally an eye to, in arguing against the reality of external existences. And indeed, the operation of perceiving objects at a distance, is so curious, and so singular, that it is not surprising, a rigid philosopher should be puzzled about it. In this case, there is a difficulty, which applies with some shew of strength, and which possibly has had weight with our author, tho' it is never once mentioned by him. It is, that no being can act but where it is, and that a body, at a distance, cannot act upon the mind, more than the mind upon it. I must candidly own, that this argument appears to evince the necessity, of some intermediate means, in the act of vision. One means is suggested by matter of fact. The image of a visible object, is painted upon the retina of the eye. And it is not more difficult to

con-

conceive, that this image may be some how conveyed to the mind, than to conceive the manner of its being painted upon the retina. This circumstance puts the operation of vision, in one respect, upon the same footing, with that of touching; both being performed by means of an impression made at the organ. There is indeed this essential difference, that the impression of touch is felt as such, whereas the impression of sight is not felt: we are not conscious of any such impression, but merely of the object itself, which makes the impression.

And here a curious piece of mechanism presents itself to our view. Tho' an impression is made upon the mind, by means of the image painted upon the retina, whereby the external object is perceived; yet nature has carefully concealed this impression from us, in order to remove all ambiguity, and to give us a distinct feeling of the object itself, and of that only. In touching and tasting, the impression made at the organ, is so closely connected with the body which makes the impression, that the perception of the impression, along with that of the body, creates no confusion nor ambiguity, the body being felt as operating where it really is. But were the impression of a visible object felt, as made at the retina, which is the organ of sight, all objects behoved to be seen as within the eye. It is doubted among naturalists, whether outness or distance is at all discoverable by sight, and whether that appearance be not the effect of experience. But bodies, and their operations, are so closely connected in place, that were we conscious of an organic impression at the retina, the mind would have a constant propensity to place the body there also; which would be a circumstance extremely perplexing, in the act of vision, as setting feeling and experience in perpetual opposition; enough to poison all the pleasure we enjoy by that noble sense.

For so short-sighted a creature as man, it is the worst reason in the world for denying
any

any well attefted fact, that we cannot account for the manner by which it is brought about. It is true, we cannot explain, after what manner it is, that, by the intervention of the rays of light, the beings, and things around us, are laid open to our view; but it is mere arrogance, to pretend to doubt of the fact, upon that account; for it is, in effect, maintaining, that there is nothing in nature, but what we can explain.

THE perception of objects at a diftance, by intervention of the rays of light, involves no inconfiftency nor impoffibility. And unlefs this could be afferted, we have no reafon nor foundation to with-hold that affent to a matter of fact, which is due to the authority of our fenfes. And after all, this particular ftep of the operation of vifion, is, at bottom, not more difficult to be conceived or accounted for, than the other fteps, of which no man entertains a doubt. It is, perhaps, not eafy to explain, how the image of an external body is painted upon the *retina tuni-*

ca,

ca. And no person pretends to explain, how this image is communicated to the mind. Why then should we hesitate about the last step, to wit the perception of external objects, more than about the two former, when they are all equally supported, by the most unexceptionable evidence. The whole operation of vision far surpasses human knowledge: but not more, than the operation of magnetism, electricity, and a thousand other natural appearances; and our ignorance of the cause, ought not to make us suspect deceit in the one case, more than in the other.

We shall conclude this subject, with the following reflection. Whether our perception of the reality of external objects, corresponds to the truth of things, or whether it be a mere illusion, is a question, which, from the nature of the thing, cannot admit of a strict demonstration. One thing is certain, that, supposing the reality of external objects, we can form no conception of their being displayed to us, in a more lively and

con-

convincing manner, than in fact is done. Why then call a thing in doubt, of which we have as good evidence, as human nature is capable of receiving? But we cannot call it in doubt, otherways than in speculation, and even then, but for a moment. We have a thorough conviction of the reality of external objects; it rises to the highest certainty of belief; and we act, in consequence of it, with the greatest security of not being deceived. Nor are we in fact deceived. When we put the matter to a trial, every experiment answers to our perceptions, and confirms us more and more in our belief,

ESSAY

ESSAY IV.
Of our IDEA *of* POWER.

THE subject proposed to be handled in the present essay is the idea of *power*, and its origin. This term is found in all languages: we talk familiarly, of a power in one body, to produce certain effects, and of a capacity in another body, to have certain effects produced upon it. Yet authors have differed strangely, about the foundation of these ideas; and, after all that has been said, it seems yet to be a matter of uncertainty, whether they are suggested by reason, by experience, or by what other means. This subject deserves our attention the more, that the bulk of useful knowledge depends upon it. Without some insight into causes and their effects, we should be a very imperfect race of beings. And, with regard to the present undertaking, this subject must not, at any rate, be overlooked; because from it, principally, is derived any knowledge

ledge we have of the Deity, as will be afterwards made evident.

Power denotes a simple idea, which, upon that account, cannot admit of a definition. But no person is, nor can be at a loss, about the meaning. Every action we perceive, gives us a notion of power; for a productive cause is implied in our perception of every action or event *; and the very idea of cause comprehends a power of producing its effect. Let us only reflect upon the perception we have, when we see a stone thrown into the air out of one's hand. In the perception of this action, are included, contiguity of the hand and stone, the motion of the person's hand with the stone in it, and the separate motion of the stone, following the other circumstances in point of time. The first circumstance is necessary, to put the man in a condition to exert his power upon the stone; the second is the actual exertion of the power; and the last is the effect produc-

ed,

---

* Essay of liberty and necessity.

IDEA OF POWER.

ed by that exertion. But these circumstances, which include both contiguity and succession, make no part of the idea of power; which is conceived or felt as an inherent property subsisting in the man, not merely when he is exerting it, but even when he is at rest. That all men have this very idea, is a fact not to be controverted. The only doubt is, whence it is derived; from what source it springs.

That reason cannot help us out, will be evident. For reason must always have some object to employ itself upon. There must be known *Data* or principles, to lead us to the discovery of things, which are connected with these *Data* or principles. But with regard to power, which makes a necessary connection betwixt a cause and its effect, we have no *Data* nor principles to lead us to the discovery. We are not acquainted with the beings and things about us, otherways than by certain qualities and properties, obvious to the external senses. Power is none of these; nor is there any

any connection which we can difcover, betwixt power and any of thefe. In a word, we have not the leaft foundation for concluding power in any body, till it once exert its power. If it be urged, that the effects produced are *Data*, from which, we can infer a caufe by a procefs of reafoning, and confequently, a power in the caufe to produce thefe effects; I anfwer, that when a new thing or quality is produced, when in general any change is brought about, it is extremely doubtful, whether, by any procefs of reafoning, we can conclude it to be an effect, fo as necefſarily to require a caufe of its exiftence. That we do conclude it to be an effect, is moft certain. But that we can draw any fuch conclufion, merely from reafon, I don't clearly fee. What leads me, I confefs, to this way of thinking, is, that men of the greateft genius have been unfuccefsful, in attempting to prove, that every thing which begins to exift, muft have a caufe of its exiftence. " Whatever is produced (fays Mr. *Locke*) " without any caufe, is produced by *nothing*;

or,

IDEA OF POWER.

" or, in other words, has *nothing* for its
" cause. But *nothing* can never be a cause,
" no more than it can be *something*." This
is obviously begging the question. To affirm that *nothing* is the cause, is taking for
granted that a cause is necessary; which is
the very point undertaken to be made out.
Doctor *Clarke*'s argument labours under the
same defect. " Every thing (he says) must
" have a cause; for if any thing wanted a
" cause, it would produce itself; that is, exist
" before it existed, which is impossible." If
a thing can exist without a cause, there is no
necessity it should produce itself, or that any
thing should produce it. In short, there does
not appear to me any contradiction in the
above proposition, that a thing may begin to
exist without a cause: and therefore, I dare
not declare the fact to be impossible. But
sense and feeling afford me a conviction, that
nothing begins to exist without a cause, tho'
reason cannot afford me a demonstration of
it. This matter will be opened afterwards.
At present, it is sufficient to observe, that the

con-

conviction in this cafe is complete, and carries so much authority with it, as scarce to admit of a bare conception, that the thing can possibly be otherways. This subject, at the same time, affords a new instance of what we have had more than once occasion to observe. Fond of arguments drawn from the nature of things, we are too apt to apply such arguments without discretion; and to call that demonstration, which, at bottom, is nothing but a conviction from sense and feeling. Our perceptions, which work silently, and without effort, are apt to be overlooked; and we vainly imagine, we can demonstrate every proposition, which we perceive to be true.

It will be pretty obvious, that the idea of power is not deducible from experience, more than from reason. We can learn nothing merely from experience, but that two objects may have been constantly conjoined in time past, such as fire and heat, the sun and light. But, in the first place, all that can

can be gathered from such facts, comes far short of our idea of cause and effect, or of a power in one body to produce some change in another. In the second place, experience, which relates only to the actions of the particular bodies we are acquainted with, cannot aid us to discover power in any body, that we have not formerly seen in action. Yet, from the very first operation of such a body, we have the perception of cause and effect, which therefore cannot be from experience. And, in the last place, as experience in no case reaches to futurity, our idea of power, did it depend upon experience, could only look backward: with regard to every new production, depending upon causes even the most familiar, we should be utterly at a loss to form any idea of power.

It being now evident, that our idea of power is not derived, either from reason or experience, we shall endeavour to trace out the true foundation of this idea. Running over the subject, the following thoughts occur

cur, which I shall set before the reader, in their natural order. As man, in his life and actions, is necessarily connected, both with the animate and inanimate world; he would be utterly at a loss to conduct himself, without some acquaintance with the beings around him, and their operations. His external senses give him all the intelligence that is necessary, not only for being, but for well-being. They discover to him, in the first place, the existence of external things. But this would not be sufficient, unless they also discovered to him their powers and operations. The sense of seeing is the principal means of his intelligence. I have explained, in a former essay, that peculiar manner of perception, by which we discover the existence of external objects. And when these are put in motion, whereby certain things follow, 'tis by another peculiar manner of perception, that we discover a relation betwixt certain objects, which makes one be termed the cause, the other the effect. I need scarce repeat again, that there is no explaining

plaining simple feelings and perceptions, otherways than by suggesting the terms which denote them. All that can be done in this case, is to request of the reader, to attend to what passes in his mind, when he sees one billiard ball struck against another, or a tree, which the wind is blowing down, or a stone thrown into the air out of one's hand. We are obviously so constituted, as not only to perceive the one body acting, and exerting its power; but also to perceive, that the change in the other body is produced by *means* of that action or exertion of power. This change we perceive to be an *effect*; and we perceive a necessary connection betwixt the action and the effect, so as that the one must unavoidably follow the other.

As I discover power in external objects, by the eye, so I discover power in my mind, by an internal sense. By one act of the will ideas are raised. By another act of the will, my limbs are put in motion. Attending to these operations, I perceive or feel the motion

tion of the limbs, and the entry of the ideas, to follow necessarily from the act of the will. In other words, I perceive or feel these to be effects, and the act of the will to be the cause.

And that this feeling is involved in the very perception of the action, without taking in either reason or experience, may be illustrated by some plain observations. There is no relation more familiar, even to children, than that of cause and effect. The first time a child lifts a bit of bread, the perception it has of this action, not only includes a conjunction of the hand with the bread, and that the motion of the latter follows the motion of the former; but it likeways includes that peculiar modification, which is exprest by a power in the hand to lift the bread. Accordingly, we find no expression more familiar among infants and rusticks, nor better understood than I *can* do this, I *can* do that. Further, as things are best illustrated by their contraries, let us put the case of a
being

IDEA OF POWER.

being, if there is such a one, who, in viewing external objects, has no idea of substance, but only of qualities; and who, in viewing motion, does not feel the change produced by it, to be an effect, or any way connected with the motion, further than as following it in point of time. It appears extremely evident, that this supposed being can never have the idea of body, or of its powers. Reason or experience can never give it the idea of body or substance, and far less of their powers.

It is very true, we cannot discover power in any object, as we discover the object itself, merely by intuition. But the moment an alteration is produced by any object, we perceive that the object has a power to produce that alteration; which leads to denominate the one a cause, and the other an effect. I don't assert that we can never be in a mistake about this matter. Children often err, by attributing an effect to one cause instead of another, or by considering that to be a cause, which is not. Miftakes of this kind are corrected by experience. But they prove the reality of the perception of power, juft as much as where our perceptions are agreeable to the truth of things.

And with regard to the fallibility of the fenfe of feeing, when it points out to us caufes and effects, the comparifon may be juftly inftituted, betwixt it and belief. The faculty which regulates belief is not infallible. It fometimes leads us into errors. Neither is the faculty infallible, by which we difcern one thing to be a caufe, another to be an effect. Yet both are exerted with fufficient certainty, to guide us through life, without many capital errors.

The author of the treatife of human nature, has employed a world of reafoning, in fearching for the foundation of our idea of power and of necèffary connection. And, after all his anxious refearches, he can make no more of it, but " That the idea of ne-
" ceffary

IDEA OF POWER. 283

"ceffary connection, *alias power* or *energy*,
"arifes from a number of inftances, of one
"thing always following another, which
"connects them in the imagination; where-
"by we can readily foretel the exiftence of
"the one from the appearance of the o-
"ther." And he pronounces, "That this
"connection can never be fuggefted from
"any one of thefe inftances, furveyed in all
"poffible lights and pofitions *." Thus
he places the effence of neceffary connection, or power, upon that propenfity, which
cuftom produces, to pafs from an object to
the idea of its ufual attendant. And from
thefe premifes, he draws a conclufion of a
very extraordinary nature, and which he himfelf acknowledges to be not a little paradox-
ical. His words are: " Upon the whole,
"neceffity is fomething that exifts in the
"mind, not in objects; nor is it poffible
"for us even to form the moft diftant idea
"of it, confidered as a quality in bodies. The
"efficacy or energy in caufes, is neither
"placed

* Philofophical effays, eff. 7.

"placed in the causes themselves, nor in the
"Deity, nor in the concurrence of these
"two principles; but belongs entirely to
"the soul, which considers the union of two
"or more objects in all past instances. 'Tis
"here that the real power of causes is plac-
"ed, along with their connection and ne-
"cessity *."

He may well admit this doctrine to be a violent paradox, because, in reality, it contradicts our natural feelings, and wages war with the common sense of mankind. We cannot put this in a stronger light than our author himself does, in forming an objection against his own doctrine. " What! the
" efficacy of causes ly in the determination of
" the mind! as if causes did not operate en-
" tirely independent of the mind, and would
" not continue their operation, even tho'
" there was no mind existent to contemplate
" them, or reason concerning them. This
" is

* Treatise of human nature, vol. 1. pag. 290, 291.

"is to reverse the order of nature, and to
"make that secondary which is really pri-
"mary. To every operation there is a pow-
"er proportioned; and this power must be
"placed on the body that operates. If we
"remove the power from one cause, we
"must ascribe it to another. But to remove
"it from all causes, and bestow it on a being
"that is noways related to the cause, or effect,
"but by perceiving them, is a gross absurdi-
"ty, and contrary to the most certain princi-
"ples of human reason †." In short, nothing is more clear, than that, from the very sight of bodies in motion, we have the
idea of power, which connects them together, in the relation of *cause* and *effect*. This
power is perceived as a quality in the acting
body, and by no means is an operation of
the mind, or an easy transition of thought
from one object to another. And therefore, flatly to deny our perception of such a
quality in bodies, as our author does, is taking upon him to contradict a plain matter of
fact,

† Pag. 294.

fact, of which all the word can give testimony. He may be at a loss, indeed, to discover the source of this perception, because he can neither derive it, nor the idea of substance, from his own principles. But it has been more than once observed, that it is too bold, to deny a fact, supported by the best evidence, merely because one is at a loss to discover the cause. At the same time, there is no manner of difficulty to lay open the foundation of these perceptions. Both of them are impressions of sight, as is clearly made out above.

And to show, that our author's account of this matter comes far short of truth, it will be plain from one or two instances, that tho' a constant connection of two objects, may, by habit or custom, produce a similar connection in the imagination; yet that a constant connection, whether in the imagination, or betwixt the objects themselves, does by no means come up to our idea of power. Far from it. In a garrison, rifon, the foldiers conftantly turn out at a certain beat of the drum. The gates of the town are opened and fhut regularly, as the clock points at a certain hour. Thefe facts are obferved by a child, grow up with him, and turn habitual during a long life. In this inftance, there is a conftant connection betwixt objects, which is attended with a fimilar connection in the imagination: yet the perfon above fuppofed, if not a changeling, never imagined, the beat of the drum to be the caufe of the motion of the foldiers; nor the pointing of the clock to a certain hour, to be the caufe of the opening or fhutting of the gates. He perceives the caufe of thefe operations to be very different; and is not led into any miftake by the above circumftances, however clofely connected. Let us put another inftance ftill more appofite. Such is the human conftitution, that we act neceffarily, upon the exiftence of certain perceptions or motives. The profpect of victuals makes a hungry man accelerate his pace. Refpect to an antient family moves him to take a wife.

An

An object of distress prompts him to lay out his money, or venture his person. Yet no man dreams a motive to be the cause of action; tho', if the doctrine of necessity hold true, here is not only a constant, but a necessary connection *.

From the instance last given, it appears, that constant connection, and the other circumstances mentioned by our author, are far from coming up to our idea of *power*. There

---

* A thought or idea, 'tis obvious, cannot be the cause of action; cannot, of itself, produce motion. After what manner then does it operate? I explain the matter thus: The power of magnetism, or any other particular power in matter, by which the body endued with the power is impelled towards other bodies, cannot operate, if there is no other body placed within its sphere of activity. But placing another body there, the magnetic body is directly impelled towards this new body. Yet the new body is not the *cause* of the motion, but only the *occasion* of it; the condition of the power being such, that the body endued with it cannot operate, but with relation to another body, within its sphere of action. Precisely, in the same manner, does the mind act, upon presenting of a thought or idea. The idea is not the *cause* of the action, but only the *occasion* of it. It is the mind which exerts the action; only 'tis so framed, that it cannot exert its powers, otherways than upon the presenting of certain perceptions to it.

There may be even a necessary connection betwixt two objects, without putting them in the relation of *cause* and *effect*, and without involving a power in the one to produce the other. Our author, then, attempts rather too bold an enterprize, when he undertakes to argue mankind out of their senses and feelings. That we have such a feeling of power, as is above described, is a fact that cannot admit of the smallest controversy. And all that is left him, would he argue with any prospect of success, is to question, whether this feeling does, in fact, correspond to the truth of things. But he will not undertake so stubborn a task, as to prove this a delusive feeling; when he must be sensible of the wonderful harmony, that subsists betwixt it and the reality of causes and their effects. We have no reason to suspect deceit in this case, more than with regard to many other senses, some of which remain to be unfolded, that are wrought into the constitution of man, for wise and good purposes, and without which, he would be a very irregular and defective being.

And were it neceffary to fay more upon a fubject, which indeed merits the utmoft attention; we have, if I miftake not, this author's own evidence for us; which I confider as no mean evidence in any cafe; and which muft be held of the greateft authority, when given againft himfelf. And this evidence he gives in his philofophical effays. For tho', in this work, he continues to maintain " That neceffity exifts only in the " mind, not in objects, and that it is not " poffible for us even to form the moft di- " ftant idea of it, confidered as a quality in " bodies;" yet, in the courfe of the argument, he more than once difcovers, that he himfelf is poffeffed of an idea of *power*, confidered as a quality in bodies, tho' he has not attended to it. Thus he obferves [*],
" That nature conceals from us, thofe pow-
" ers and principles, on which the influ-
" ence

[*] London edition, pag. 58.

IDEA OF POWER. 291

"ence of objects entirely depends." And of these powers and principles, he gives several apt instances, such as a power or quality in bread to nourish; a power by which bodies persevere in motion. This is not only owning an idea of power as a quality in bodies, but also owning the reality of this power. In another passage †, he observes, "That the particular powers, by which all "natural operations are performed, never ap- "pear to the senses;" and "that experi- "ence does not lead us to the knowledge "of the secret power by which one object "produces another." What leads us to the knowledge of this secret power, is not at present the question. But here is the author's own acknowledgment, that he has an idea of a power in one object to produce another; for he certainly will not say, that he is here making use of words, without having any ideas annexed to them. In one passage in particular *, he talks distinctly and explicitly of "A power in one object, by which
"it

† Pag. 72.   * Pag. 121.

" it infallibly produces the other, and operates
" with the greateſt certainty and ſtrongeſt
" neceſſity." No maſter of language can give
a deſcription of power, conſidered as a quality in bodies, in more apt or more expreſ
ſive terms. So difficult it is to ſtifle, or to
diſguiſe natural feelings and ſentiments *.

If the foregoing arguments have not prevailed, may not the following argument
hope for ſucceſs? Figure the ſimpleſt of all
caſes; a man riſing from his ſeat, to walk
through the room; and try to analyſe the
perception of this ſimple event. In the firſt
place, is the man active or paſſive? Is he
moved, or does he move himſelf? No mortal is at a loſs to underſtand theſe queſtions;
and no mortal is at a loſs to anſwer them.
We have a diſtinct perception or feeling, that
the man is not moved, but moves; or, which
is the ſame, moves himſelf. Let us examine, in the next place, what is involved in
the perception or feeling we have, when we
ſee

---

* Naturam expellas furca, tamen uſque recurret.

see this man walking. Do we not say familiarly, does not a child say, that he *can* walk? And what other thing do we mean by this expression, than that he has a *power* to walk? Does not the very idea of walking include in it a power to walk? In this instance, our author, unhappily for his argument, has neither contiguity nor succession to recur to, for explaining his idea of power, imperfect as it is. And therefore, with regard to this instance, he must either admit, that we have an idea of power, considered as a quality in objects, or take upon him to deny, that we have any idea of power at all: for it is evident, that the idea of power, when it comprehends only a single object, can never be resolved into a connection in the imagination, betwixt two or more objects. We have thus the feeling of power from every action, be it of the simplest kind that can be figured. And having once acquired the idea of power exerted by an animal, to put itself in motion, we readily transfer that idea to the actions of bodies, animate and inanimate, upon

on each other. And, after all, with due regard to an author of very acute parts, I cannot help obferving, that there is, perhaps, not one idea of all the train, which is more familiar to us, or more univerfal, than the idea of power.

Having thus afcertained the reality of our idea of power, as a quality in bodies, and traced it to its proper fource, I fhall clofe this effay with fome obfervations upon caufes and their effects. That we cannot difcover power in any object, otherways than by feeing it exert its power, is above obferved. Therefore, we can never difcover any object to be a caufe, otherways than by the effect produced. But with regard to things caufed or produced, the cafe is very different. For we can difcover an object to be an effect, after the caufe is removed, or when it is not at all feen. For inftance, no one is at a lofs to fay, that a table or a chair is an effect produced. A child will ask, who made it? We perceive every event, every

new

IDEA OF POWER. 295

new object, to be an effect or production, the very conception of which involves the idea of a cause. Hence the maxim, "That nothing can fall out, nothing begin to exist, without a cause;" in other words, "That every thing which begins to exist must have a cause:" a maxim universally recognised, and admitted by all mankind as self-evident. Nor can this be attributed to experience. The feeling is original, regarding singular objects and events, the causes of which are utterly unknown, not less than objects and events, which depend upon familiar causes. Children and rusticks are conscious of this feeling, equally with those who have the most consummate experience of nature, and its operations *.

FURTHER, the perception we have of any object, as an effect, includes in it the feeling of a cause proportioned to the effect. If the object be an effect properly adapted to some end, the perception of it necessarily includes

* See the essay upon liberty and necessity, pag. 88.

cludes an intelligent defigning caufe. If the effect be fome good end brought about by proper means, the perception necefsarily includes a defigning and benevolent caufe. Nor is it in our power, by any fort of conftraint, to vary thefe feelings, or to give them a different modification from what they have by nature. It may be in our power to conceive, but it is not in our power to believe, that a fine piece of painting, a well wrote poem, or a beautiful piece of architecture, can ever be the effect of chance, or of blind fatality. The fuppofition, indeed, fo far as we can difcover, does not involve any inconfiftency in the nature of things. It may be poffible, for any reafon we have to the contrary, that a blind and undefigning caufe may be productive of excellent effects. But our fenfes difcover, what reafon does not, that every object, which appears beautiful as adapted to an end or purpofe, is the effect of a defigning caufe ; and that every object, which appears beautiful as fitted to a good end or purpofe, is the effect of a defigning caufe;

cause; and that every object, which appears beautiful as fitted to a good end or purpose, is the effect of a designing and benevolent cause. We are so constituted, that we can entertain no doubt of this, if we would. And, so far as we gather from experience, we are not deceiv'd.

ESSAY V.
Of our KNOWLEDGE of FUTURE EVENTS.

WHILE we are tied to this globe, some knowledge of the beings around us, and of their operations, is neceſſary; becauſe, without it, we ſhould be utterly at a loſs how to conduct ourſelves. This ſubject is handled in two former eſſays. But were our knowledge limited to this ſubject, it would not be ſufficient for our well-being, and ſcarce for our preſervation. It is likeways neceſſary, that we have ſome knowledge of future events; for about theſe we are moſtly employed. A man will not ſow, if he has not a proſpect of reaping: he will not build a houſe, if he has not ſome ſecurity, that it will ſtand firm for years. Man is poſſeſt of this valuable branch of knowledge: he can foretel future events. There is no doubt of the fact. The difficulty only is, what are the means employed in making the discovery. It is, indeed, an established maxim, that the course of nature continues uniformly the same; and that things will be as they have been. But, from what premises we draw this conclusion, is not obvious. Uniformity in the operations of nature, with regard to time past, is discovered by experience. But of future time, having no experience, the maxim assuredly cannot be derived from that source. Neither will reason help us out. It is true, the production of one thing by another, even in a single instance, implies a power; and this power is necessarily connected with its effect. But as power is an internal property, not discoverable but by the effects produced, we can never, by any chain of reasoning, conclude, power to be in any body, except in the instant of operation. The power, for ought we know, may be at an end from that very instant. We cannot so much as conclude, from any deduction of reason, that this earth, the sun, or any one being, will exist to-morrow. And, supposing their future existence

istence to be discoverable by reason, we are not so much acquainted with the nature or essence of any one thing, as to discover a necessary connection betwixt it and its powers, that the one subsisting, the other must also subsist. There is nothing so easy to conceive, as that the most active being, shall at at once be deprived of all its activity: and a thing that may be conceived, can never be proved inconsistent or impossible. An appeal to past experience, will not carry us through. The sun has afforded us light and heat from the beginning of the world. But what reason have we to conclude, that its power of giving light and heat must continue; when it is as easy to conceive powers to be limited in point of time, as to conceive them perpetual? If to help us out here, we have recourse to the wisdom and goodness of a Supreme Being, as establishing permanent general laws; the difficulty is, that we have no *Data*, from whence to conclude, in the way of reasoning, that these general laws must continue invariably the
same

same without end. It is true, the conclusion is actually made, but it must be referred to some other source. For reasoning will not aid us, more than experience does, to draw any one conclusion, from past to future events. It is certain, at the same time, that the uniformity of nature's operations, is a maxim admitted by all mankind. Tho' altogether unassisted either by reason or experience, we never have the least hesitation to conclude, that things will be as they have been; in so much that we trust our lives and fortunes upon this conclusion. I shall endeavour to trace out the principle, upon which this important conclusion is founded. And this subject will afford, 'tis hoped, a fresh instance of the admirable correspondence, which is discovered betwixt the nature of man, and his external circumstances. What is already made out, will lead us directly to our point. If our conviction of the uniformity of nature, is not founded upon reason nor experience, it can have no other foundation but sense and feeling. The fact truly ly is, that we are so constituted, as, by a necessary determination of nature, to transfer our past experience to futurity, and to have a direct perception or feeling of the constancy and uniformity of nature. This perception or feeling must belong to an internal sense, because it evidently has no relation to any of our external senses. And an argument, which has been more than once stated in the foregoing essays, will be found decisive upon this point. Let us suppose a being, which has no perception or notion of the uniformity of nature: such a being will never be able to transfer its past experience to futurity. Every event, however conformable to past experience, will come equally unexpected to this being, as new and rare events do to us; tho' possibly without the same surprise.

This sense of constancy and uniformity in the works of nature, is not confined to the subject above handled, but displays itself, remarkably, upon many other objects. We

We have a conviction of a common nature in beings, which are similar in their appearances. We expect a likeness in their constituent parts, in their appetites, and in their conduct. We not only lay our account with uniformity of behaviour, in the same individual, but in all the individuals of the same species. This principle has such influence, as even to make us hope for constancy and uniformity, where experience would lead us to the opposite conclusion. The rich man never thinks of poverty, nor the distressed of relief. Even in this variable climate, we cannot readily bring ourselves to believe, that good or bad weather will have an end. Nay, it governs our notions in law-matters, and is the foundation of the maxim, " That " alteration or change of circumstances is " not to be presumed." Influenced by the same principle, every man acquires a certain uniformity of manner, which spreads itself upon his thoughts, words and actions. In our younger years, the effect of this principle is less remarkable, being opposed by a

variety

variety of passions, which, as they have different, and sometimes opposite tendencies, occasion a fluctuation in our conduct. But, so soon as the heat of youth is over, this principle, acting without counter-balance, seldom fails to bring on a punctual regularity in our way of living, which is extremely remarkable in most old people.

Analogy is one of the most common sources of reasoning; the force of which is universally admitted. The conviction of every argument founded on analogy, arises from this very sense of uniformity. Things similar, in some particulars, are presumed to be similar in every particular.

In a word, as the bulk of our views and actions have a future aim, some knowledge of future events is necessary, that we may adapt our views and actions to natural events. To this end, the Author of our nature has done two things. He has established a constancy and uniformity in the operations of nature. And he has impressed upon our minds, a conviction or belief of this constancy and uniformity, and that things will be as they have been.

ESSAY

ESSAY VI.

Of our Dread *of* Supernatural Powers *in the* Dark.

A VERY flight view of human nature is sufficient to convince us, that we were not dropt here by accident. This earth is fitted for man, and man is fitted for inhabiting this earth. By means of inflinctive faculties, we have an intuitive knowledge of the things that furround us; at leaft of fuch things by which we may be affected. We can difcover objects at a diftance. We difcern them in their connection of caufe and effect; and their future operations are laid open, as well as their prefent. But in this grand apparatus of inflinctive faculties, by which the fecrets of nature are difclofed to us, one faculty feems to be with-held; tho' in appearance the moft ufeful of all; and that is, a faculty to difcern, what things are noxious, and what are friendly. The moft poifonous fruits have fometimes the faireft colours;

and

and the favage animals partake of beauty with the tame and harmlefs. And when other particulars are inquir'd into, it will be found, by induction, that man has no original feeling of what is falutary to him, and what is hurtful.

It is natural to inquire why this inftinct is with-held, when it appears to be the defign of nature, to furnifh us plentifully with inftincts, for the difcovery of ufeful truths. With regard to this matter, it is too bold an undertaking for man to dive into all the fecrets of his maker. We ought to reft contented with the numerous inftances we have of good order and good purpofe, which muft afford us a rational conviction, that good order and good purpofe take place univerfally. At the fame time, a rational account may be fuggefted of this matter. We have a conviction, that there is nothing redundant or fuperfluous in the operations of nature. Different means are never afforded us to bring about the fame end. Experience, so far as it can go, is given us for acquiring knowledge; and instinct only, where experience cannot aid us. 'Tis true, instinct is a more compendious way of discovering useful truths. But man was intended an active being, and therefore left to his own industry, as much as possible.

Man then is placed in this world, amidst a great variety of objects, the nature and tendency of which are unknown to him, otherways than by experience. In this situation, he would be in perpetual danger, had he not some faithful monitor, to keep him constantly upon the watch against harm. This monitor is the propensity he has to be afraid of new objects; such especially which have no peculiar beauty to raise his desire. A child, to whom all nature is strange, dreads the approach of every object; and even the face of man is frightful to it. The same timidity and suspicion may be observed in travellers, who converse with strangers, and meet with unknown appearances. Upon the first sight of an herb or fruit, we apprehend the worſt, and ſuſpect it to be noxious. An unknown animal is immediately conceived to be dangerous. The more rare phænomena of nature, the cauſes of which are unknown to the vulgar, never fail to ſtrike them with terror. From this induction, it is clear, that we dread unknown objects. They are always ſurveyed with an emotion of fear, 'till experience diſcovers them to be harmleſs.

This dread of unknown objects, is ſuppoſed to enter into the conſtitution of all ſenſitive beings, but is moſt remarkable in the weak and defenceleſs. The more feeble and delicate the creature is, the more ſhy and timorous it is obſerved to be. No creature is, by nature, more feeble and delicate than man; and this principle is to him of admirable uſe, to keep him conſtantly upon his guard, and to balance the principle of curioſity, which is prevalent in man above all other creatures, and which, left to itſelf, would often betray him into fatal accidents.

The

POWERS IN THE DARK.

The dread of unknown objects is apt to fire the imagination, so as to magnify their supposed evil qualities and tendencies. For it is a well known truth, that passion has a wonderful effect upon the imagination. The less we know of a new object, the greater liberty we take, to dress it up in frightful colours. The object is forthwith conceived to have all those dreadful qualities, which are suggested by the imagination; and the same terror is raised, as if those qualities were real and not imaginary *.

Again, where the new and unknown objects have any thing dreadful in appearance, this circumstance, joined with our natural propensity to dread unknown objects, will raise terror even in the most resolute. If the evils, dreaded from such objects, are known neither in quality nor degree; the imagination, being under no restraint, figures the greatest evils, both in kind and magnitude, that can be conceived. Where no immediate harm ensues, the mind, by the impulse

* See essay upon belief.

pulse it has received, transports itself into futurity, and imagines the strange forms to be presages of direful calamities. Hence it is, that the uncommon phænomena of nature, such as comets, eclipses, earthquakes, and the like, are, by the vulgar, held as forerunners of uncommon events. Grand objects make a deep impression upon the mind, and give force to that passion which occupies it at the time. The above appearances being uncommon, if not altogether new, dispose the mind to terror; which, aided by the emotion arising from the grandeur of the objects, produces great agitation, and a violent apprehension of danger.

The strongest and most familiar instance of our natural propensity to dread unknown objects, is the fear that seizes many young persons in the dark; which is a phænomenon that has not been accounted for, with any degree of satisfaction. Light disposes the mind to chearfulness and courage. Darkness, on the contrary, depresses the mind, and disposes

it

it to fear. Any object alarms the mind, when it is already prepared by darkness, to receive impressions of fear. The object, which, in the dark, is seen but obscurely, leaves the heated imagination at full liberty, to bestow upon it the most dreadful appearance. This phantom of the imagination, conceived as a reality, unhinges the mind, and throws it into a fit of distraction. The imagination, now heated to the highest degree, multiplies the dreadful appearances to the utmost bounds of its conception. The object becomes a spectre, a devil, a hobgoblin, something more terrible than ever was seen or described.

A very few accidents of this kind, having so powerful an effect, are sufficient to introduce an association between darkness and malignant powers. And when once this association is formed, there is no occasion for the appearance of an object to create terror. Frightful ideas croud into the mind, and augment the fear, which is occasioned by darkness. The imagination becomes ungovernable,

able, and converts thefe ideas into real appearances.

That the terror occafioned by darknefs, is entirely owing to the operations of the imagination, will be evident from a fingle reflection, that in company no fuch effect is produced. A companion can afford no fecurity againft fupernatural powers. But a companion has the fame effect with funfhine, to chear the mind, and preferve it from gloominefs and defpondency. The imagination is thereby kept within bounds, and under due fubjection to fenfe and reafon.

ESSAY

ESSAY VII.

Of our Knowledge *of the* Deity.

THE arguments *a priori* for the existence and attributes of the Deity, are urged, with the greatest shew of reason, in the sermons preached at Boyle's lectures. But the sermons upon this subject, tho' they command my strictest attention, never have gained my heart. On the contrary, they always give me a sensible uneasiness; the cause of which I have been at a loss to discover, tho' now I imagine I can explain it. Such deep metaphysical reasoning, if it afford any conviction, is surely not adapted to the vulgar and illiterate. Is the knowledge of God, then, reserved for persons of great study and deep thinking? Is a vail thrown over the eyes of the rest of mankind? This thought always returned upon me, and gave me pain. If there really exists a being, who made, and who governs the world; and, if it be his purpose to display himself to his rational creatures; it is not

not consistent with any idea we can form of the power and wisdom of this being, that his purpose should be defeated; which plainly is the case, in a great measure, if he is only to be discovered, and but obscurely, by a very small part of mankind. At the same time, to found our knowledge of the Deity solely upon reasoning, is not agreeable to the analogy of nature. We are not left to gather our duty by abstract reasoning, nor indeed by any reasoning. It is engraved upon the table of our hearts. We adapt our actions to the course of nature, by mere instinct, without reasoning, or even experience. Therefore, if we can trust to analogy, we ought to expect, that God will discover himself to us, in some such manner, as may take in all mankind, the vulgar and illiterate, as well as the deep thinking philosopher.

If these abstruse arguments, however, are relished by the learned and speculative, 'tis so far well. I cannot help acknowledging, that they afford me no conviction, at least, no solid and permanent conviction. We know little about the nature of things, but what we learn from a strict attention to our own nature. That nothing can begin to exist without a cause, is sufficiently evident from sense and feeling *. But that this can be demonstrated by any argument *a priori*, drawn from the nature of things, I have not observed †. And if demonstration fail us in the very outsetting, we cannot hope for its assistance in the after steps. If any one being can begin to exist without a cause, every being may; upon which supposition, we never can hope for a demonstration, that any one being must be eternal. But, if this difficulty shall be surmounted, we have another to struggle with. Admitting that something has existed from all eternity, I find no *Data* to determine *a priori*, whether this world has existed of itself from all eternity, in a constant succession of causes and effects; or whether it be an effect produced by

---

* See the essay of our idea of power, towards the close.
† See the same essay at the beginning.

by an Almighty Power. It is indeed hard to conceive a world eternal and self-exiftent, where all things are carried on by blind fate, without defign or intelligence. And yet I can find no demonftration to the contrary. If we can form any obfcure notion of one intelligent being, exifting from all eternity, it appears not more difficult to form a notion of a fucceffion of beings, with or without intelligence; or a notion of a perpetual fucceffion of caufes and effects.

In fhort, difficulties prefs both ways. But, thefe difficulties, when examined, do not arife from any inconfiftency in our ideas. They are occafioned, merely, by the limited capacity of the mind of man. We cannot comprehend an eternity of exiftence. It is too bulky an object. It eludes our grafp. The mind is like the eye. It cannot take in an object that is very great or very little. This, plainly is the fource of our difficulties, when we attempt fpeculations fo remote from common apprehenfion. Abftract reafoning upon fuch a fubject, muft
lead

OF THE DEITY.

lead into endless perplexities. It is indeed less difficult to conceive one eternal unchangeable being who made the world, than to conceive a blind chain of causes and effects. At least, we are disposed to the former, as being more agreeable to the imagination. But as we cannot find any inconsistency in the latter supposition, we cannot justly say that it is demonstrably false.

GIVE me leave to add, that to bring out such abstruse and intricate speculations into any clear and persuasive light, is at any rate scarce to be expected. And if, after the utmost straining, they remain obscure and unaffecting, it is evident to me, that they must have a bad tendency. Persons of a peevish and gloomy cast of mind, finding no conviction from that quarter, will be fortified in their propensity to believe that all things happen by blind chance; that there is no wisdom, order or harmony in the government of this world; and consequently that there is no God.

BEING

320 OUR KNOWLEDGE

Being therefore little follicitous about arguments *a priori*, for the exiftence of a Deity, which are not proportioned to the capacity of man, I apply myfelf with zeal and chearfulnefs, to fearch for the Deity in his works; for by thefe we muft difcover him, if he has thought proper to make himfelf known. And the better to manage the inquiry, I fhall endeavour to make out three propofitions; 1*ft*, That if there is a being who is the maker and governor of the world, it is agreeable to any notions we can form of his government, that he fhould make fome difcovery of himfelf to his intelligent creatures. 2*dly*, That in fact he has done fo. And 3*dly*, That he has done fo in a manner agreeable to the nature of man, and analogous to his other operations.

There certainly cannot be a more difcouraging thought to man, than that the world was formed by a fortuitous concourfe of atoms, and that all things are carried on by blind impulfe. Upon that fuppofition,

he

he can have no security for his life; nor for his continuing to be a moral agent and an intelligent creature, even for a moment. Things have been carried on with regularity and order. But chance may, in an instant, throw all things into the most horrid and dismal confusion. We can have no solid comfort in virtue, when it is a work of mere chance; nor can we justify our reliance upon the faith of others, when the nature of man rests upon so precarious a foundation. Every thing must appear gloomy, dismal and disjointed, without a Deity to unite this world of beings into one beautiful and harmonious system. These considerations, and many more that will occur upon the first reflection, afford a very strong conviction, if there is a wise and good Being, who superintends the affairs of this world, that he will not conceal himself from his rational creatures. Can any thing be more desirable, or more substantially useful, than to know, that there is a Being from whom no secrets are hid, to whom our good works are acceptable, and even the good purposes of our hearts; and whose government, directed by wisdom and benevolence, ought to make us rest secure, that nothing does or will fall out, but according to good order? This sentiment, rooted in the mind, is an antidote to all misfortune. Without it, life is at best but a confused and gloomy scene.

AND this leads to a different consideration, which makes our knowledge of a benevolent Deity of the greatest importance to us. Tho' natural and moral evil are far from prevailing in this world, yet so much of both is scattered over the face of things, as to create some degree of doubt, whether there may not be a mixture of chance, or of ill-will, in the government of this world. But, once supposing the superintendency of a good being, these evils are no longer considered as such. A man restrains himself from unlawful pleasures, tho' the restraint gives him pain. But then he does not consider this pain, as an evil to repine at. He submits to it it voluntarily and with satisfaction, as one does to grief for the loss of a friend; being conscious that it is *right* and *fit* for him to be so affected. In the same manner, he submits to all the evils of this life. Having confidence in the good government of the Deity, he is persuaded that every thing happens for the best, and therefore that it is his duty to submit to whatever happens. This unfolds a scene so enlivening, and so productive of chearfulness and good humour, that we cannot readily think, if there is a benevolent Deity, that he will with-hold from his creatures so invaluable a blessing.

Man, at the same time, by his taste for beauty, regularity and order, is fitted for contemplating the wisdom and goodness displayed in the frame and government of this world. These are proper objects of admiration and joy. It is not agreeable to the ordinary course of nature, that man should be endowed with an affection, without having a proper object to bestow it upon.

on. And as the providence of the Deity is the highest object of this affection, it would be unnatural, that he should be kept in ignorance of it.

These, I admit, are but probable reasons for believing, that, if there is a benevolent Deity, it must be his intention to manifest himself to his creatures: but they carry a very high degree of probability, which leaves little room for doubt. At the same time, tho' it should be our fate, to search in vain for this object of our affection, we ought not however to despair, and, in that despair, to conclude there is no God. Let us but reflect, that he has not manifested himself to all his creatures. The brutes apparently know nothing of him. And should we be disappointed in this search, the worst we can conclude, is, that for good and wise purposes, which we cannot dive into, he has thought proper to with-hold himself also from us. We certainly have no reason to convert our ignorance into an argument
against

OF THE DEITY.

against his existence. Our ignorance brings us only a step lower, and puts us, so far, upon a footing with the brute creation.

The second and important branch of our disquisition, is, to ascertain this fact, that there is a Deity, and that he has manifested himself to us. I request only attention of my reader, and not any unreasonable concession. In a former essay *, two propositions are made out. The first is, that every thing which has a beginning, is perceived as a *production* or *effect*, which necessarily involves the idea of a *cause*. The second, that we necessarily transfer to the cause, whatever of contrivance or design is discovered in the effect. Considering a house, garden, picture or statue in itself, it is perceived as beautiful. If we attend to these objects in a different view, as things having a beginning, we perceive them to be effects, involving the idea of a cause. If again we consider them as artfully contrived to answer certain purposes, we perceive them to be the workman-

ship

* Of our idea of power.

ship of some person of skill. Nor are we deceived in these perceptions. Upon examination, we find, that they correspond to truth and reality.

But not only are these objects perceived as effects, which we afterwards learn, from experience, to be the production of man. Natural objects, such as plants and animals, as well as all other objects which once were not, are also perceived as effects, or as the production of some cause. The question will always recur, how came it here? who made it? what is the cause of its existence?

We are so accustomed to human arts, that every work of design and use will be attributed to man. But what if it exceed his known powers and faculties? This supposition does not alter the nature of our feelings; but only leads us to a different cause, and, in place of man, to determine upon some superior power. If the object be considered as an effect, it necessarily involves the idea

OF THE DEITY. 327

idea of a cauſe. And the cauſe cannot be man, if the object of our perception be an effect far ſurpaſſing the power of man. This train of thinking leads us directly to our point. Attend but to the anatomy of the meaneſt plant: ſo much of art and of curious mechaniſm is diſcovered in it, that it muſt be the production of ſome cauſe, far ſurpaſſing the power and intelligence of man. The ſcene opens more and more, when, paſſing from plants to animals, we come to man, the moſt wonderful of all the works of nature. And when, at laſt, we take in, at one view, the natural and moral world, full of harmony, order and beauty; happily adjuſted in all its parts to anſwer great and glorious purpoſes; there is, in this grand production, neceſſarily involved, the perception of a cauſe, unbounded in power, intelligence and goodneſs.

Thus it is, that the Deity has manifeſted himſelf to us, by the means of principles wrought into our nature, which muſt infallibly

libly operate, upon viewing objects in their relation of cauſe and effect. We diſcover external objects by their qualities of colour, figure, ſize and motion. In the perception of theſe qualities, connected after a certain manner, is comprehended, the feeling of the ſubſtance or thing, to which theſe qualities belong. At the ſame time, we perceive this ſubſtance or thing, ſuppoſing it to have a beginning of exiſtence, to be an effect produced by ſome cauſe; and we perceive the powers and properties of this cauſe from its effects. If there is an aptitude in the effect to ſome end, we attribute to the cauſe, intelligence and deſign. If the effect produced be ſome thing that is good in itſelf, or that has a tendency to ſome good end or pupoſe, we attribute goodneſs to the cauſe, as well as intelligence and deſign. And this we do, not by any proceſs of reaſoning, but merely by perception and feeling. The Deity has not left his exiſtence to be gathered from ſlippery and far-fetched arguments. We have but to open our eyes, to receive impreſſions

of

of him almoſt from every thing we perceive. We diſcover his being and attributes, in the ſame manner that we diſcover external objects. We have but to appeal to our own perceptions; and none but thoſe, who are ſo ſtubbornly hypothetical, as to deny the exiſtence of matter, againſt the evidence of their ſenſes, can, ſeriouſly and deliberately, deny the exiſtence of the Deity. In fine, there is a wonderful harmony eſtabliſhed betwixt our perceptions and the courſe of nature. We truſt to our perceptions, for the exiſtence of external objects, and their paſt, preſent and future operations. We truſt to theſe perceptions by the neceſſity of our nature, and, upon experience, find ourſelves not deceived. Our perception of the Deity, is as diſtinct and authoritative, as that of external objects. And tho' here, we cannot have experience to appeal to, the want of experience can never afford an argument againſt the authority of any perception, where, from the nature of the thing, there can be no experience. It is ſufficient for conviction, that our perceptions in general correspond to the truth of things, wherever there is an opportunity to try them by experience; and therefore, we can have no cause to doubt of our perceptions in any case, where they are not contradicted by experience.

So far the Deity is discoverable, by every person who goes but one step beyond the surface of things, and their mere existence. We may indeed behold the earth in its gayest dress, the heavens in all their glory, without having any perception, other than that of beauty, something in these objects that pleases and delights us. Many pass their lives, brutishly involved in the gross pleasures of sense, without having any feeling, at least, any strong or permanent feeling, of the Deity; and possibly, this in general is the case of savages, before they are humanized by society and government. But the Deity cannot be long a secret from those who are accustomed to any degree of reflection. No sooner are we enabled to relish beauties of

the

the second and third clafs *; no fooner do we acquire a tafte for regularity, order, defign, and good purpofe, than we begin to perceive the Deity, in the beauty of the operations of nature. Savages who have no confiftent rule of conduct, who act by the blind impulfe of paffion and appetite, and who have only a glimmering of the moral fenfe, are but ill qualified to difcover the Deity in his works. If they have little or no perception of a juft tenor of life, of the dignity of behaviour, and of the beauty of action, how fhould they perceive the beauty of the works of creation, and the admirable harmony of all the parts, in the great fyftem of things? Being confcious of nothing but diforder and fenfual impulfe within, they cannot be confcious of any thing better without them. Society teaches mankind felf-denial, and improves the moral fenfe. Difciplined in fociety, the tafte for order and regularity unfolds itfelf by degrees. The focial affections

---

* See the effay upon the foundation and principles of the law of nature.

ons gain the ascendant, and the morality of actions gets firm possession of the mind. In this improved state, the beauty of the creation makes a strong impression; and, we can never cease admiring the excellency of that cause, who is the author of so many beautiful effects. And thus, to society we owe all the blessings of life, and, particularly, the knowledge of the Deity, that most inestimable branch of human knowledge.

Hitherto we have gone no further, than to point out the means by which we discover the Deity, and his attributes of power, wisdom and goodness. So far are we carried by those wonderful principles in our nature, which discover the connection betwixt cause and effect, and from the effect discover the powers and properties of the cause. But there is one attribute of the Supreme Being, of the most essential kind, which remains to be unfolded. It is, what commonly passes under the name of self-existence, that he must have existed for ever;

ever; and consequently, that he cannot be considered as an effect, to require a cause of his existence; but, on the contrary, without being caused, that, mediately, or immediately, he is the cause of all other things. A principle, we have had occasion, more than once, to mention, will make this evident, *viz.* that nothing can begin to exist without a cause. Every thing which comes into existence, and once was not, is, by a necessary determination of our nature, perceived as an effect, or as a production; the very conception of which, involves an adequate cause. Now, if every thing has a beginning, one being, at least, to wit, that which first came into existence, must be an effect or production without a cause, which is a direct inconsistency. If all beings had a beginning, there was a time, when the world was an absolute void; upon which supposition, it is intuitively certain, that nothing could ever have come into existence. This proposition we feel to be true, and our feeling affords us, in this case, a more solid conviction,

viction, than any demonstration can do. One being, therefore, must have existed from all eternity, who, as he is not an effect or production, cannot possibly be indebted for his existence to any other being. At the same time, as we can have no foundation for supposing the existence of more eternal beings than one, this one being must be the Deity; because, all other beings, mediately, or immediately, owe their existence to him. All other beings, as they are supposed to be produced in time, must have a cause of their existence, and, by the supposition, there can be no other cause but this eternal Being. The bulk of mankind, probably, in their notions of the Deity, scarce comprehend this attribute of self-existence. A man must be used, a good deal, to abstract reasoning, who of himself discovers this truth. But it is not difficult to explain it to others, after it is discovered. And it deserves well to be inculcated; for, without it, our knowledge of the Deity must be extremely imperfect. His other attributes of power, wisdom and goodnefs,

OF THE DEITY. 335

nefs, are, in fome meafure, communicated to his creatures; but his attribute of felf-exiftence makes the ftrongeft oppofition imaginable, betwixt him and his creatures.

A few words will fuffice upon the third propofition, which, in a good meafure, is already explained. The effence of the Deity is far beyond the reach of our comprehenfion. Were he to exhibit himfelf to us, in broad day-light, it is not a thing fuppofable, that he could be reached by any of our external fenfes. The attributes of felf-exiftence, wifdom, goodnefs and power, are purely intellectual. And therefore, fo far as we can comprehend, there are no ordinary means to acquire any knowledge of the Deity, but by his works. And indeed, by means of that fenfe which difcovers caufes from their effects, he has manifefted himfelf to us in a fatisfactory manner, liable to no doubt nor error. And after all, what further evidence can we defire, when the evidence we have of his exiftence is little inferior to that we

have

have of our own exiſtence? Impreſſions or perceptions ſerve us for evidence in both caſes*. Our own exiſtence, indeed, is, of all facts, that which concerns us moſt; and, therefore, of our own exiſtence we ought to have the higheſt certainty. Next to it, we have not, as it appears to me, a greater certainty of any matter of fact, than of the exiſtence of the Deity. 'Tis, at leaſt, equal to the certainty we have of external objects, and of the conſtancy and uniformity of the operations of nature, upon the faith of which our whole ſchemes of life are adjuſted.

The arguments *a poſteriori,* which have been urged for the Being and attributes of the Deity, are generally defective. There is always wanting one link of the chain, to wit, that peculiar principle, upon which is founded our knowledge of cauſes and their effects. But the calm perceptions, turning habitual by frequent repetition, are apt to be overlooked

* See the eſſay upon the idea of ſelf and perſonal identity.

looked in our reasonings. Many a proposition is rendered obscure, by much laboured argument, for the truth of which, we need but appeal to our own perceptions. Thus, we are told, that the frame and order of the world, the wisdom and goodness displayed in every part of it, are an evident demonstration of the Being of a God. I confess, these things afford us full conviction of his Being. But, laying aside perception and feeling, I should be utterly at a loss, by any sort of reasoning, to conclude the existence of any one thing, from that of any other thing. In particular, by what process of reasoning, can we demonstrate this conclusion to be true, that order and beauty must needs proceed from a designing cause? It is true, the idea of an effect involves the idea of a cause. But how does reason make out, that the thing we name an effect, may not exist of itself, as well as what we name a cause? If it be urged, that human works, where means are apparently adjusted to an end, and beauty and order discovered,

covered, are always known to be the effects of intelligence and design. True, they are: and as far as I have experience, I believe the fact to be so. But, where experience fails me, I desire to know, by what step, what link in the chain of reasoning, am I to connect my past experience with this inference, that in every case, I ought to form the same conclusion? If it be said, that nature prompts us to judge of similar instances, by former experience; this is giving up reason and demonstration, to appeal to that very feeling, on which, I contend, the evidence of this truth must entirely rest. All the arguments *a posteriori*, may be resolved into this principle; which, no doubt, has had its due influence upon the writers who handle the present subject; tho', I must be allowed to say, it has not been explained, nor, perhaps, sufficiently understood by them; whereby, all of them have been led into the error, of stating as demonstrative reasoning, what is only an appeal to our senses. They reason, for example, upon the equality of males and females,

OF THE DEITY.

males, and hold the infinite odds against this equality, to be a demonstration, that matters cannot be carried on by chance. This, considered as mere reasoning, does not conclude; for, besides that chance is infinite in its varieties, there may be, some blind fatality, some unknown cause, in the nature of things, which produces this uniformity. But tho' reason cannot afford demonstration in this case, sense and feeling afford conviction. The equality of males and females, is one of the many instances which we know and feel to be the effects of a designing cause; and of which we can no more entertain a doubt, than of our own existence. The same principle, which unfolds to us the connection of causes and their effects, in the most common events, discovers this whole universe to stand in the relation of an effect to a supreme cause.

To substitute feeling in place of reason and demonstration, may seem to put the evidence of the Deity upon too low a footing.

But

But human reason is not so mighty an affair, as philosophers vainly pretend. It affords very little aid, in making original discoveries. The comparing of things together, and directing our inferences from feeling and experience, are its proper province. In this way, reason gives its aid, to lead us to the knowledge of the Deity. It enlarges our views of final causes, and of the prevalence of wisdom and goodness. But the application of the argument from final causes, to prove the existence of a Deity, and the force of our conclusion, from beautiful and orderly effects to a designing cause, are not from reason, but from an internal light, which shows things in their relation of cause and effect. These conclusions rest entirely upon sense and feeling; and it is surprising, that writers should overlook what is so natural, and so obvious. But the pride of man's heart, makes him desire to extend his discoveries, by dint of reasoning. For reasoning is our own work. There is merit in acuteness and penetration; and we are better

pleased

pleased to assume merit to ourselves, than humbly to acknowledge, that, to the most important discoveries, we are directly led by the hand of the Almighty.

Having unfolded that principle, upon which I would rest the most important of all truths; objections must not be overlooked, such as appear to have weight: and I shall endeavour to give these objections their strongest effect, which ought to be done in every dispute, and which becomes more strictly a duty, in handling a subject, where truth is of the utmost importance.

Considering the above argument on all sides, I do not find, that it can be more advantageously combated, than by opposing to it, the eternity and self-existence of the world, governed by chance or blind fatality. 'Tis above admitted to be very difficult, by any abstract reasoning, to prove the inconsistency of this supposition. But we feel the inconsistency; for the frame and conduct of
this

this world, contain in them, too much of wisdom, art and foresight, to admit of the supposition of chance or blind fatality. We are necessarily determined, by a principle in our nature, to attribute such effects to some intelligent and designing cause. Supposing this cause to be the world itself, we have, at least, got free of the supposition of chance and blind fatality. And, if the world be a being, endued with unbounded power, intelligence and benevolence, the world is the being we are in quest of; for we have no other idea of the Deity, but of an eternal and self-existent being, endued with power, wisdom and goodness. But the hypothesis, thus reformed, still contradicts our perceptions. The world is made up of parts, separable, and actually separated. The attributes of unbounded power, intelligence and benevolence, do certainly not belong to this earth, and as little to the sun, moon or stars, which are not conceived to be even voluntary agents. Therefore, these attributes must belong to a Being, who made the earth, sun,

sun, moon and stars, and who connects the whole together in one system.

A second objection may be, that the above reasoning, by which we conclude the eternity and self-existence of one Being who made this world, does not necessarily infer such a conclusion, but only, an eternal succession of such beings; which may be reckoned a more natural supposition, and more agreeable to our feelings, than the idea of one eternal self-existent Being, without any cause of his existence.

In matters so profound, it is difficult to form ideas with any degree of accuracy. I have observed above, that it is too much for man, to grasp, in his idea, an eternal Being, whose existence, upon that account, cannot admit of the supposition of a cause. To talk, as some of our metaphysical writers do, of an absolute necessity in the nature of the Being, as the cause of his existence, is mere jargon. For we can conceive nothing more clearly,

clearly, than that the cause must go before the effect, and that the cause cannot possibly be in the effect. But, however difficult it may be, to conceive one eternal Being, without a cause of its existence; it is not less difficult, to conceive an eternal succession of beings, deriving their existence from each other. For, tho' every link be supposed a production, the chain itself exists without a cause, as well as one eternal Being does. Therefore, an eternal succession of beings, is not a more natural supposition, than one eternal self-existent Being. And taking it in a different light, it will appear a supposition much less natural, or rather altogether unnatural. Succession in existence, implying the successive annihilation of particulars, is indeed a very natural conception. But then, it is intimately connected with frail and dependent beings, and cannot, without the utmost violence to the conception, be applied to the Maker of all things, to whom, we naturally ascribe, perpetual existence, and every other perfection. And therefore, as

this

this hypothefis of a perpetual fucceffion, when applied to the Deity, is deftitute of any fupport from reafon or experience, and is contradicted by every one of our natural feelings, there can be no ground for adopting it.

The noted obfervation of Lucretius, that *primos in orbe deos fecit timor*, may be objected; as it will be thought unphilofophical, to multiply caufes for our belief of a Deity, when fear alone muft have that effect. For my part, I have little doubt of the truth of the obfervation, taking it in its proper fenfe, that fear is the foundation of our belief of invifible malevolent powers. For it is evident, that fear can never be the caufe of our belief of a benevolent Deity. I have unfolded, in another effay*, the caufe of our dread of malevolent invifible powers. And I am perfuaded, that nothing has been more hurtful to religion, than the irregular propenfity in our nature, to dread fuch powers. Superficial thinkers are apt to confound thefe

---

* Of our dread of fupernatural powers in the dark.

these phantoms of the imagination, with the objects of our true and genuine perceptions. And finding so little reality in the former, they are apt to conclude the latter, also, to be a fiction. But, if they gave any sort of deliberate attention, they would soon learn, by the assistance of history, if not by original feeling, to distinguish these objects, as having no real connection with each other. Man, in his original savage state, is a shy and timorous animal, dreading every new object, and attributing every extraordinary event, to some invisible malevolent power. Led, at the same time, by mere appetite, he has little idea of regularity and order, of the morality of actions, or of the beauty of nature. In this state, it is no wonder, he multiplies his invisible malevolent powers, without entertaining any notion of a supreme Being, the Creator of all things. As man ripens in society, and is benefited by the goodwill of others, his dread of new objects gradually lessens. He begins to perceive regularity and order in the course of nature. He

becomes

OF THE DEITY.

becomes sharp-sighted, in discovering causes from effects, and effects from causes. He ascends gradually, thro' the different orders of beings, and their operations, till he discovers the Deity, who is the cause of all things. And when we run over the history of man, it will be found to hold true in fact, that savages, who are most possest with the opinion of evil spirits, have, of all people, the least idea of a Deity; and, that as all civilized nations, without exception, entertain the firm belief of a Deity, so the dread of evil spirits wears out in every nation, in proportion to their gradual advances in social intercourse.

And this leads to a reflection, which cannot fail to have universal influence. Man, in a savage and brutish state, is hurried away by every gust of passion, and by every phantom of the imagination. His powers and faculties are improved by education, and good culture. He acquires deep knowledge in the nature of things, and learns accurately to distinguish truth from falsehood. What more

more satisfying evidence can we require, of the truth of our perceptions of the Deity, than to find these perceptions prevalent, in proportion, as mankind improve in the arts of life? These perceptions go hand in hand with the rational powers. As man increases in knowledge, and in the discerning faculties, his perceptions of the Deity become proportionally more strong, clear and authoritative. The universal conviction of a Deity, which has, without exception, spread through all civilized nations, cannot possibly be without a foundation in nature. To insist that it may, is to insist, that an effect may be without an adequate cause. Reason cannot be an adequate cause; because, our reasonings upon this subject, must, at best, be abstruse, and beyond the comprehension of the bulk of mankind. Our knowledge, therefore, of the Deity, must be founded on our perceptions and feelings, which are common to mankind. And it is agreeable to the analogy of nature, that God should discover himself to his rational creatures

tures after this manner. If this subject be involved in any degree of obscurity, writers are to blame, who, in a matter of so great importance, ought to give no quarter to inaccuracy of thought or expression. But it is an error, common to the bulk of writers, to substitute reason for feeling. The faculty of perception, working silently, and without effort, is generally overlookt. And we must find a reason for every thing we judge to be true; tho' the truth of the proposition often depends, not upon reasoning, but upon mere feeling. It is thus, that morality has been brought under some obscurity, by metaphysical writers; and it is equally to be regreted, that the knowledge of the Deity has been brought under obscurity, by the same sort of writers.

Having settled the belief of a Deity upon its proper basis, we shall proceed to take a general view of the attributes, which belong to that great Being; and first,

Of the Unity of the Deity.

WITH regard to this, and all the other attributes of the Deity, it ought to be no difcouraging reflection, that we cannot attain an adequate idea of them. The Deity is too grand an object, to be comprehended, in any perfect manner, by the human mind. We have not words nor ideas, which any way correfpond to the manner of his exiftence. Should fome good angel undertake to be our inftructor, we would ftill be at a lofs, to form a diftinct conception of it. Power, intelligence and goodnefs, are attributes which we can comprehend. But with regard to the nature of the Deity in general, and the manner of his exiftence, we muft be fatisfied, in this mortal ftate, to remain much in the dark. The attribute of *Unity*, is what, of all, we can have the leaft certainty about, by the light of nature. It is not inconfiftent, that there fhould be two or more beings of the very higheft order, whofe effence and actions are fo regulated

by

by the nature of the beings themselves, as to be altogether concordant and harmonious. In truth, the nature of the Divine Being is so far out of our reach, that we must be absolutely at a loss, to apply to it *unity* or *multiplicity*. This property applies to numbers, and to individual things, but we know not that it will apply to the Deity. At the same time, if we may venture to judge, of a matter so remote from common apprehension, we ought to conclude in favours of the attribute of *unity*. We perceive the necessity of admitting one eternal Being; and it is sufficient, that there is not the smallest foundation from sense or reason, to suppose more than one.

Of

Of the Power *and* Intelligence *of the* Deity.

THESE two attributes I join together, because the same reflection will apply to both. The wisdom and power, which must necessarily be supposed, in the creation and government of this world, are so far beyond the reach of our comprehension, that they may justly be stiled *infinite*. We can ascribe no bounds to either: and we have no other notion of *infinite*, but that, to which we can ascribe no bounds.

Of the Benevolence *of the* Deity.

THE mixed nature of the events, which fall under our observation, seems, at first sight, to point out a mixed cause, partly good and partly evil. The author of " phi-
" losophical essays concerning human un-
" derstanding," in his eleventh essay, " of
" the practical consequences of natural reli-
" gion," puts in the mouth of an Epicurean philosopher, a very shrewd argument against the benevolence of the Deity. The sum of it is what follows. " If the cause be known
" only by the effect, we never ought to af-
" sign to it any qualities, beyond what are
" precisely requisite to produce the effect.
" Allowing therefore God to be the Author
" of the existence and order of the universe;
" it follows, that he possesses that precise
" degree of power, intelligence and benevo-
" lence, which appears in his workmanship."
And hence, from the present scene of things, apparently so full of ill and disorder, it is

concluded, " That we have no foundation
" for ascribing any attribute to the Deity,
" but what is precisely commensurate with
" the imperfection of this world." With
regard to mankind, an exception is made. " In
" works of human art and contrivance, it is
" admitted, that we can advance from the
" effect to the cause, and returning back from
" the cause, that we conclude new effects,
" which have not yet existed. Thus, for in-
" stance, from the sight of a half-finished
" building, surrounded with heaps of stones
" and mortar, and all the instruments of
" masonry, we naturally conclude, that the
" building will be finished, and receive all
" the farther improvements, which art can be-
" stow upon it. But the foundation of this
" reasoning is, plainly, that man is a being
" whom we know by experience, and whose
" motives and designs we are acquainted
" with, which enables us to draw many in-
" ferences, concerning what may be expect-
" ed from him. But did we know man on-
" ly from the single work or production,
" which

OF THE DEITY. 355

"which we examine, we could not argue in
"this manner; because our knowledge of
"all the qualities which we ascribe to him,
"being, upon that supposition, derived from
"the work or production, it is impossible
"they could point any thing farther, or be
"the foundation of any new inference."

Supposing reason to be our only guide
in these matters, which is supposed by this
philosopher in his argument, I cannot help
seeing his reasoning to be just. It appears
to be true, that by no inference of reason,
can I conclude any power or benevolence in
the cause, beyond what is displayed in the
effect. But this is no wonderful discovery.
The philosopher might have carried his argument
a greater length. He might have observed,
even with regard to a man I am perfectly
acquainted with, that I cannot conclude,
by any chain of reasoning, he will finish
the house he has begun. 'Tis to no
purpose to urge his temper and disposition.
For, from what principle of reason can I infer,

fer, that these will continue the same as formerly? He might further have observed, that the difficulty is greater, with regard to a man I know nothing of, supposing him to have begun the building. For what foundation have I, to transfer the qualities of the persons I am acquainted with, to strangers? This surely is not performed by any process of reasoning. There is still a wider step, which is, that reason will not help me out in attributing to the Deity, even that precise degree of power, intelligence and benevolence, which appears in his workmanship. I find no inconsistency in supposing, that a blind and undesigning cause may be productive of excellent effects. It will, I presume, be difficult to produce a demonstration to the contrary. And supposing, at the instant of operation, the Deity to have been endued with these properties, can we make out, by any argument *a priori*, that they are still subsisting in him? Nay, this same philosopher might have gone a great way further, by observing, when any thing comes into existence,

OF THE DIETY.

istence, that, by no process of reasoning, can we so much as infer any cause of its existence.

But happily for man, where reason fails him, perception and feeling come to his assistance. By means of principles implanted in our nature, we are enabled to make the above conclusions and inferences, as, at full length is made out, in some of the foregoing essays. More particularly, power, discovered in any object, is perceived as a permanent quality, like figure or extension *. Upon this account, power discovered by a single effect, is considered, as sufficient, to produce the like effects without end. Further, great power may be discovered from a small effect; which holds even in bodily strength; as where an action is performed readily, and without effort. This is equally remarkable in wisdom and intelligence. A very short argument may unfold correctness of judgment and a deep reach. The same

* Essay upon our knowledge of future events.

same holds in art and skill. Examining a slight piece of workmanship done with taste, we readily observe, that the artist was equal to a greater task. But it is most of all remarkable in the quality of benevolence. For even, from a single effect produced by an unknown cause, which appears to be accurately adapted to some good purpose, we necessarily attribute to this cause, benevolence, as well as power and wisdom *. It is indeed but a weak perception, which arises from a single effect: but still, it is a clear and distinct perception of pure benevolence, without any mixture of malice; for such contradictory qualities, are not readily to be ascribed to the same cause. There may be a difficulty indeed, where the effect is of a mixt nature, partly evil, partly good; or where a variety of effects, having these opposite characters, proceed from the same cause. Such intricate cases cannot fail to embarass us. But, as we must form some sentiment, the resolution of the difficulty plainly

* Essay of our idea of power, at the close.

plainly is, that we muſt aſcribe benevolence or malevolence to the cauſe, from the prevalence of the one or other quality in the effects. If evil makes the greateſt figure, we perceive the cauſe to be malevolent, notwithſtanding of oppoſite inſtances of goodneſs. If, upon the whole, goodneſs is ſupereminent, we perceive the cauſe to be benevolent; and are not moved by the croſs inſtances of evil, which we endeavour to reconcile, as we can, to pure benevolence. It is, indeed, true, that where the oppoſite effects nearly balance each other, our perception cannot be entire upon the ſide of benevolence or malevolence. But, if good or evil greatly preponderate, the weight in the oppoſite ſcale goes for nothing: the perception is entire upon one ſide or other. Becauſe it is the tendency of our perceptions, to reject a mixt character made up of benevolence and malevolence, unleſs, where it is neceſſarily preſt home upon us, by an equality of oppoſite effects.

Such

Such are the conclusions, that we can with certainty draw, not indeed from reason, but from sense and feeling. So little are we acquainted with the essence and nature of things, that we cannot establish these conclusions upon any argument *a priori*. Nor would it be of great benefit to mankind, to have these conclusions demonstrated to them; few having either leisure or genius to deal in such profound speculations. It is more wisely ordered, that they appear to us intuitively certain. We feel that they are true, and our feelings have full authority over us. This is a solid foundation for our conviction of the benevolence of the Deity. If, from a single effect, pure benevolence in the cause can be perceived or felt; what doubt can there be, of the pure benevolence of the Deity, when we survey his works, pregnant with good-will to mankind? Innumerable instances, of things wisely adapted to good purposes, give us the strongest feeling, of the goodness, as well as wisdom, of the Deity; which is joined with the firmest
per-

OF THE DEITY.

persuasion of constancy and uniformity in his operations. A few cross instances, which to us, weak-sighted mortals, may appear of evil tendency, ought not, and cannot make us waver. When we know so little of nature, it would be surprising, indeed, if we should be able to account for every event, and its final tendency. Unless we were let into the counsels of the Almighty, we can never hope to unravel all the mysteries of the creation.

As we cannot say too much upon a subject, which is of all the most interesting, I shall add some other considerations, to justify our belief of the pure benevolence of the Deity. And, in the first place, I venture to lay it down for a truth, that pure malice, is a principle not to be found in human nature. The benevolence of man, is, indeed, often checked and counteracted by jealousy, envy, and other selfish passions. But, these are distinct from pure malice; for, pure goodness is not opposite to self-interest, but to satisfaction in the misfortunes and miseries of others. Now, the independent and all-sufficient nature of the Deity, sets him above all suspicion of being liable to envy, or the pursuit of any interest, other than the general interest of his creatures. Wants, weakness, and opposition of interests, are the causes of ill-will and malice among men. From all such influences, the Deity must be exempted. And therefore, unless we suppose him less perfect than the creatures he has made, we cannot readily suppose, that there is any degree of malice in his nature.

There is a second consideration, which has always afforded me great satisfaction. Did natural evil prevail in reality, as much as it does in appearance, we must expect, that the enlargement of natural knowledge, should daily discover new instances of bad, as well as of good intention. But the fact is directly otherways. Our discoveries ascertain us more and more of the benevolence

of

of the Deity, by unfolding beautiful final causes without number; while the appearances of evil intention gradually vanish, like a mist, after the sun breaks out. Many things are now found to be curious in their contrivance, and productive of good effects, which formerly appeared useless, or, perhaps, of evil tendency. And, in the gradual progress of learning, we have the strongest reason to expect, that many more discoveries, of the like kind, will be made hereafter. This very consideration, had we nothing else to rely on, ought to make us rest upon the assurance which our feelings give us of the benevolence of the Deity; without giving way to the perplexity of a few cross appearances, which, in matters so far beyond our comprehension, ought to be ascribed to our own ignorance, and, by no means, to any malevolence in the Deity.

I shall satisfy myself with suggesting but one other observation, that, inferring a mixed nature in the Deity, from events which

which cannot be clearly reconciled to benevolence, is at beſt, new moulding the Manichean ſyſtem, by ſubſtituting, in place of it, one really leſs plauſible. For, I can, with greater facility, form a conception of two oppoſite powers, governing the univerſe, than of one power, endued with great goodneſs, and great malevolence; which are principles repugnant to each other.

It thus appears, that our conviction of this attribute of pure benevolence, has a wide and ſolid foundation. It is impreſſed upon us by a natural feeling, by every diſcovery we make in the ſcience of nature, and by every argument which is ſuggeſted by reaſon and reflection. There is but one objection of any weight, which can be moved againſt it, ariſing from the difficulty of accounting for natural and moral evil. It is obſerved above, that this objection, however it may puzzle, ought not to ſhake our faith in this attribute; becauſe, an argument from ignorance, can never be a convincing argument
in

OF THE DEITY.

in any cafe; and this therefore, in its ftrongeft light, appears but in the fhape of a difficulty, not of a folid objection. At the fame time, as the utmoft labour of thought is well beftowed upon a fubject, in which mankind is fo much interefted, I fhall proceed to fuggeft fome reflections, which may tend to fatisfy us, that the inftances commonly given of natural and moral evil, are not fo inconfiftent with pure benevolence, as, at firft fight, may be imagined.

One preliminary point muft be fettled, which, I prefume, will be admitted without much hefitation. It certainly will not be thought, in any degree, inconfiftent with the pure benevolence of the Deity, that the world is filled with an endlefs variety of creatures, gradually afcending in the fcale of being, from the moft groveling, to the moft glorious. To think otherways, would be in effect to think, that all inanimate beings ought to be endued with life and motion, and that all animate beings ought to be angels. If, at firſt view, it ſhall be thought, that infinite power and goodneſs cannot ſtop ſhort of abſolute perfection in their operations, and that the work of creation muſt be confined to the higheſt order of beings in the higheſt perfection; this thought will ſoon be corrected, by conſidering, that, by this ſuppoſition, a great void is left, which, according to the preſent ſyſtem of things, is filled with beings, and with life and motion. And, ſuppoſing the world to be repleniſhed with the higheſt order of beings, created in the higheſt degree of perfection, it is certainly an act of more extenſive benevolence, to complete the work of creation, by the addition of an infinity of creatures leſs perfect, than to leave a great blank, betwixt beings of the higheſt order, and nothing.

The imperfection then of a created being, abſtractly conſidered, is no impeachment of any of the attributes of the Deity, whether power, wiſdom, or benevolence. And if ſo, neither can pain, abſtractly conſidered,

dered, be an impeachment, so far as it is the natural and necessary consequence of imperfection. The government of the world is carried on by general laws, which produce constancy and uniformity in the operations of nature. Among many reasons for this, we can clearly discover one, which is unfolded in a former essay*, that, were not nature uniform and constant, men, and other sensible beings, would be altogether at a loss how to conduct themselves. Our nature is adjusted to these general laws, and must, therefore, be subjected to all their varieties, whether beneficial or hurtful. We are made sensible beings, and therefore equally capable of pleasure and pain. And it must follow, from the very nature of the thing, that delicacy of feeling, which is the source of much pleasure, may be equally the source of much pain. It is true, we cannot pronounce it to be a contradiction, that a being should be susceptible of pleasure only, and not of pain. But no argument can be founded upon this supposition, but what will conclude,

that

---

* Of our knowledge of future events.

that a creature, such as man, ought to have no place in the scale of beings; which surely will not be maintained. For it is still better, that man be as he is, than not be at all. It is further to be observed in general, that aversion to pain, is not so great, at least in mankind, as to counterbalance every other appetite. Most men would purchase an additional share of happiness, at the expence of some pain. And therefore, it can afford no argument against the benevolence of the Deity, that created beings are found liable to pain, from their nature and condition, supposing, in the main, their life to be comfortable. Their state is still preferable to that of inanimate matter, capable neither of pleasure nor pain.

Thus then, it appears, even from a general view of our subject, that natural evil affords no argument against the benevolence of the Deity. And this will still appear in a stronger light, when we go to particulars. It is fully laid open in the first essay, that the
social

social affections, even when most painful, are accompanied with no degree of aversion, whether in the feeling itself, or in the after reflection. We value ourselves the more, for being so affected; being conscious that it is *right* and *meet* to be so affected. Distresses, therefore, of this sort, cannot be called evils, when we have no aversion to them, and do not repine at them. And if these be laid aside, what may be justly termed natural evils, will be reduced within a small compass. They will be found to proceed necessarily, and by an established train of causes and effects, either from the imperfection of our nature, or from the operation of general laws. Pain is not distributed through the world, blindly, or with any appearance of malice; but ends, proportions and measures, are observed in the distribution. Sensible marks of good tendency, are conspicuous, even in the harshest dispensations of Providence, as well as in its general laws: and the good tendency of these general laws, is a sure pledge of benevolence, even in those instances, where we may be at a lofs about their application. One thing is certain, that there is in man, a natural principle to fubmit to thefe general laws and their confequences. And, were this principle cultivated, as it ought to be, mankind would have the fame confcioufnefs of rectitude of conduct, in fubmitting to the laws of the natural world, that they have in fubmitting to the laws of the moral world, and would as little repine at the diftreffes of the one kind, as at thofe of the other.

But we cannot do juftice to the argument, unlefs we proceed further, to fhow, that pain and diftrefs are productive of manifold good ends, and that the prefent fyftem could not well be without them. In the firft place, pain is neceffary, as a monitor of what is hurtful and dangerous to life. Every man is trufted with the care of his own prefervation; and he would be ill qualified for this truft, were he left entirely to the guidance of reafon. He would die for want of food,

were

OF THE DEITY.

were it not for the pain of hunger. And but for the pain arising from fear, he would precipitate himself, every moment, into the most destructive enterprises. In the next place, pain is the great sanction of laws, both human and divine. There would be no order nor discipline in the world, without it. In the third place, the distresses and disappointments, which arise from the uncertainty of seasons, from the variable tempers of those we are connected with, and from other cross accidents, are wonderfully well adapted to our constitution, by keeping our hopes and fears in perpetual agitation. Man is an active being, and is not in his element, but when in variety of occupation. A constant and uniform tenor of life, without hopes or fears, however agreeable in itself, would soon bring on satiety and disgust. Pain therefore is necessary, not only to enhance our pleasures, but to keep us in perpetual motion. And it is needless to observe, a second time, that, to complain of man's constitution in this respect, is, in other words, to complain, that there is such a creature as man in the scale of being. And to mention but one other thing, pain and distress have a wonderful tendency to advance the interests of society. Grief, compassion and sympathy, are strong connecting principles, by which every particular man is made subservient to the general good of the whole species.

I shall close this branch of my subject with a general reflection, which is reserved to the last place, because, in my apprehension, it brings the argument for the benevolence of the Deity, within a very narrow compass. When we run over what we know of the formation and government of this world, the instances are without number, of good intention, and of consummate wisdom, in adjusting things to good ends and purposes. And it is equally true, that, as we advance in knowledge, scenes of this kind multiply upon us. This observation is enforced above. But I have now to observe, that there is not a single instance to be met with,
which

which can be juftly afcribed to malevolence or bad intention. Many evils may be pointed out; evils at leaft as to us. But when the moft is made of fuch inftances, they appear only to be the confequences of general laws, which regard the whole more than particulars; and therefore are no marks of malevolence in the author and governor of the world. Were there any doubt about the tendency of fuch inftances, it would be more rational to afcribe them to want of power, than want of benevolence, which is fo confpicuous in other inftances. But we cannot rationally afcribe them to either, but to the pre-eftablifhed order and conftitution of things, and to the neceffary imperfection of the nature of all created beings. And, after all, laying the greateft weight upon thefe natural evils, that can reafonably be demanded, the accompt ftands thus. Inftances without number of benevolence, in the frame and government of this world, fo direct and clear, as not to admit of the fmalleft dubiety. On the other fide, natural evils are ftated, which,

at

at best, are very doubtful instances of malevolence, and may be ascribed, perhaps obscurely, to another cause. In balancing this accompt, where the evil appearances are so far out numbered by the good, why should we hesitate a moment to ascribe pure benevolence to the Deity, and to conclude these evils to be necessary defects in a good constitution; especially when it is so repugnant to our natural feelings, to ascribe great benevolence, and great malevolence, to the same being?

It will be observed, that in answering the above objection to the benevolence of the Deity, I have avoided urging any argument from our future existence; tho' it affords a fruitful field of comfort, greatly overbalancing the transitory evils of this life. But I should scarce think it fair reasoning, to urge such topics upon this subject; which would be arguing in a circle. Because the benevolence of the Deity is the only solid principle, from whence we can infer a future existence.

HAVING

OF THE DEITY.

Having dispatched what occurred upon natural evil, we come now, to consider moral evil as an objection against the benevolence of the Deity. And, some writers urge this objection so far, as to conclude, that God is the cause of moral evil, since he has given man a constitution, by which, moral evil, does, and must abound. It is certainly no satisfying answer to this objection, that moral evil is the necessary consequence of human liberty, when human liberty must, at best, appear a doubtful fact. And even admitting of human liberty, it is a very possible supposition, that man might have been endued with a moral sense, so lively and strong, as to be absolutely authoritative over his actions. Waving, therefore, the argument from human liberty, we must look about for a more solid answer to the objection; which will not be difficult, when we consider this matter, as laid down in a former essay*. It is there made out, 'tis hoped to the satisfaction of the reader, that human actions

---

* Essay upon liberty and necessity.

tions, are, all of them, directed by general laws, which have an operation, not lefs infallible, than thofe laws have, which govern mere matter; that the feeling we have of liberty, does not correfpond to the truth of things; and, that our peculiar manner of conceiving human actions, as right or wrong, and as praife or blame worthy, is wholly founded on this deceitful feeling. The final caufe of this fingular feeling, is alfo there laid open; that it is happily adjufted to the nature of man, as an imperfect being, and tends to promote virtue in an eminent degree. This difcovery affords a folid anfwer to an objection, which, fo far as I know, has not hitherto received any good anfwer. And it is, that the objection refts entirely upon a falfe fuppofition, as if human actions were feen in the fame light by the Deity, in which they are feen by men. A feeling, which is not agreeable to the truth of things, tho' wifely ordered to correct an imperfect conftitution in man, cannot be afcribed to a perfect being. The Deity perceiving all things

as

as they are, without difguife, knows, that what is termed moral evil in the language of man, is, as well as moral good, the refult of general laws, and of a neceffary connection betwixt caufes and their effects. Every thing poffeffes its proper place in his plan. All our actions contribute equally to carry on the great and good defigns of Providence; and, therefore, there is nothing which in his fight is evil; at leaft, nothing which is evil upon the whole.

Considering the objection in the above light, which is the true one, it lofes its force. For it certainly will not be maintained as an argument againft the goodnefs of the Deity, that he endued mankind with a fenfe of moral evil; which, in reality, is one of the greateft bleffings beftowed upon him, and which eminently diftinguifhes him from the brute creation.

But if, now, the objection be turned into another fhape, and it be demanded, Why was not every man endued with fo ftrong a fenfe of morality, as to be completely authoritative over all his principles of action, which would prevent much remorse to himself, and much mischief to others? It is answered, first, that this would not be sufficient for an exact regularity of conduct, unless man's judgment of right and wrong were also infallible. For, as long as we differ about what is *yours*, and what is *mine*, injustice must be the consequence, in many instances, however innocent we be. But, in the next place, to complain of a defect in the moral sense, is to complain, that we are not perfect creatures. And, if this complaint be well founded, we may, with equal justice, complain, that our understanding is but moderate, and that, in general, our powers and faculties are limited. Why should it be urged as an objection, that the moral sense is imperfect, when all our senses, internal and external are imperfect? In short, if this complaint be, in any measure, just, it must go the length, as above observed, to prove, that it is not consistent with the benevolence of the Deity, to create such a being as man.

CONCLUSION.

WE have thus gone through a variety of subjects, not without labour and expence of thought. And now, like a traveller, who, after examining the different parts of a country, ascends some eminence to review the whole; let us refresh ourselves, by looking back, and enjoying the discoveries we have made.

The subject of these essays is Man. We have formed no imaginary schemes for exalting, or for depressing his nature. The inquiry has been, whither his capacities and powers suit his present circumstances, and fit him for acting a proper part in life. We begin with examining some of the great springs of action. Upon accurate scrutiny, it is found, that self-love, or desire of good, is not our sole principle of action; but, that we are furnished, besides, with a variety of impelling powers. Mingled in society, for
the

the convenience of mutual help, it is necessary, that we feel for each other. But as the feeling for another's sorrow, cannot but be painful; here is traced, an admirable contrivance, to reconcile us to this virtuous pain; by taking off that aversion to pain, which, in all other cases, is an over-ruling principle. This explains a seemingly strange phænomenon, that we should seek entertainment, from representations, which immerse us in the deepest affliction. From man as a social, we proceed to man as a moral agent. We find him sensible of beauty, in different ranks and orders; and eminently sensible of it, in its highest order, that of sentiment, action and character. But the sense of moral beauty, is not alone sufficient. The importance of morality requires some stronger principle to guard it; some checks and restraints from vice, more severe than mere disapprobation. These are not wanting. To the sense of beauty, is superadded a sense of obligation; a feeling of *right* and *wrong*, which constitutes a law within us. This law enjoins

the

CONCLUSION.

the primary virtues, those which are essential to society, under the strictest sanctions. Pain, the strongest monitor, is here employed, to check transgression: whilst in the sublimer, more heroic parts of virtue, where strict obligation ends, pleasure is employed to reward the performance. To nothing are we prompted as a duty, for which we are not first prepared, by some inward principle. An exact proportion is maintained betwixt the strength of our internal principles, and their usefulness. From self, the object of our most essential principles, affection spreads thro' all the connections we have with others, whether formed by natural ties, founded on gratitude, or created by sympathy with the distressed; till, among persons indifferent and unknown, affection is gradually lost. Arrived at that point, where benevolence would vanish by the distance of the object, nature has an admirable artifice for reviving its force; by directing it on the abstract idea of a Public and a Whole: which, tho' faint and obscure in the conception, is yet equal to any

of

of our ideas, in force and energy. Man is, in this manner, furnished for acting a proper and useful part, in the system to which he belongs. But this system could not be regulated upon any pre-adjusted plan: the actions of man could not proceed with any order, nor be subject to any government; unless all were necessarily determined by motives. At the same time, man could not well conceive himself to be a moral, without conceiving himself, also, to be a free, agent. Hence the necessity of giving his mind a peculiar cast; in which, we cannot but discern the brightest characters of designing wisdom. By having his practical ideas, and his moral feelings, form'd upon an imaginary state of liberty, conscience exerts its power over him, with full authority; and scope is given, for a far richer and more diversified scene of action, than the perpetual consciousness of necessity could have admitted. Having shown, that morals are established on an immovable foundation, we proceed to show, by what inward powers we are led to

the

CONCLUSION.

the knowledge and belief of some of the most necessary truths; particularly that which it most imports us to know, the existence of the Deity. To this we pave the way, by a full preparation of reasoning. We first consider the nature of that act of the mind, which is termed *belief*; of which the immediate foundation is the testimony of our senses. If the testimony they give to the real existence of a material world, be a mere illusion, as some have held, all belief founded on our own feelings, is at an end. Hence there appears a necessity for establishing the authority of our senses. And here we find full satisfaction. For, in other cases, where there is any thing like artifice in the conduct of nature, means are afforded, both of discovering the truth, and of discovering the end, for which artifice is made use of, to conceal the truth. She never deceives us in vain. But, in the case of external existences, we find nothing, after the strictest scrutiny, but presumptions, hypotheses and fallacious reasonings, opposed to the clearest testimony, which

nature

nature can give. Dispersing with no great labour, that philosophic dust, which sceptics have raised about material substance, we find it no more difficult to be conceived, than qualities; both being equally displayed to us, by a peculiar modification of the sense of sight. But belief is not more solidly founded upon our external senses, than upon our internal feelings. Not the greatest sceptic ever doubted of his own personal identity, continued thro' the successive periods of life; of his being the same man this year, he was the last: which, however, is a discovery made by no reasoning; resting wholly upon a simple feeling, or inward sense and consciousness of the fact. Upon a like foundation rests our belief of cause and effect. No relation is more familiar, nor sooner takes hold of the mind, than this. Yet certain it is, that no reasoning, no experience, can discover the power or energy of what we term a cause, when we attempt to trace it to its source. It is necessary for the well-being of man, first, that he should perceive the objects, which ex-

ist

CONCLUSION.

ift around him; and next, that he fhould perceive them in their true ftate, not detached and loofe, but as caufes and effects, as producing and produced. Nature has furnifhed us with external fenfes for the perception of objects, not only as fimply exifting, but as exifting thus related to each other. Nor, without fuch faculties, could we ever have attained the idea of caufe and effect. The fame provifion is made by nature, in another cafe, not lefs remarkable than the former. Our fenfes can only inform us of objects as prefently exifting. Yet nothing is more common, than from our knowledge of the prefent, and our experience of the paft, to reafon to the future. Now all reafonings about futurity, which have fuch extenfive influence on our conduct, would be utterly deftitute of a foundation, were we not endowed with a fenfe of uniformity and conftancy in the operations of nature. A fecret inftinct founds this conclufion, that the future will be like the paft. Thus there is eftablifhed, a marvelous harmony betwixt our inward feelings, and the courfe of external events.

events. In the above mentioned inſtances, we attribute to our boaſted reaſon, what, in truth, is performed by ſenſe or inſtinct. Without knowing it to be ſuch, we truſt to it. We act upon its informations, with equal confidence, as we do upon the cleareſt concluſions of reaſon: and, in fact, it does not oftner deceive us. Nature thus moſt effectually provides for our inſtruction, in things moſt neceſſary to be known. But this is not all. We purſue the argument into a ſort of intuitive demonſtration of the Deity. He has not left us to collect his exiſtence from abſtract or uncertain arguments; but has made us feel, that he exiſts. When external objects are preſented to our view, ſome are immediately diſtinguiſhed to be effects, not by any proceſs or deduction of reaſoning, but merely by ſight, which gives us the perception of cauſe and effect. Juſt in the ſame manner, this whole world is ſeen, or diſcovered, to be an effect produced by ſome inviſible deſigning cauſe. This argument cannot be invalidated, without introducing

CONCLUSION.

cing universal scepticism; without overthrowing all that is built upon the feelings, which, in many capital instances, govern our judgments and actions; and without obliging us, to doubt of those things, of which no man ever doubted. For, as in viewing an external object, a particular modification of the sense of sight, includes the idea of substance, as well as of quality; as a natural feeling makes us conceive some things as effects, to be ascribed to a proper cause; as, from experience of the past, instinct prompts us to judge of the future; in fine, as, by the feeling of identity, the reader is conscious of being the same person he was when he began to read: as all these conclusions, I say, upon which mankind rest with the fullest assurance, are the dictates of senses external and internal; in the very same way, and upon the same evidence, we conclude the existence of a first Supreme Cause. Reason, when applied to, gives us all its aid, both to confirm the certainty of his being, and to discover his perfections. From effects so great, and so good, as those we see through the universe, we necessarily infer the cause to be both great and good. Mixed or imperfect qualities cannot belong to him. The difficulties from apparent evil, are found capable of a satisfactory solution. All the general laws of the universe, are confessedly wise and good. Pain is found not to be useful only, but necessary in the present system. If this be an argument of an imperfect state, yet must it not be admitted, that, somewhere in the scale of existence, an imperfect order of beings must be found? And why not man such a being? unless we extravagantly demand, that, to prove the benevolence of the Deity, all the possible orders of being should be advanced to the top of the scale, and all be left void and waste below: no life, no existence allowed, except what is perfect. The more of nature is explored and known, the less of evil appears. New discoveries, of wisdom, order and good intention, have always kept pace with increasing learning and knowledge: an intimation, not obscure, of its being owing to our imperfect

CONCLUSION.

perfect discoveries and bounded views, that evil is supposed to take place at all. Now, when we consider all these things in one view; so many striking instances of final causes; such undeniable proofs both of wise design, and skilful execution; in place of indulging cold distrust of the great universal cause, are we not raised to the highest admiration! Is there not somewhat in this subject, that has power to kindle a noble enthusiasm? And that will justify us for attempting a higher strain?

" For do not all these wonders, *O Eternal*
" *Mind*! Sovereign Architect of all! form a
" hymn to thy praise? If in the dead inani-
" mate works of nature, thou art seen; if
" in the verdure of the fields, and the azure
" of the skies, the ignorant rustic admires thy
" creative power; how blind must that man
" be, who, looking into his own nature,
" contemplating this living structure, this
" moral frame, discerns not thy forming
" hand? What various and complicated machinery

"chinery is here! and regulated with what
"exquisite art! Whilst man pursues happi-
"ness as his chief aim, thou bendest self-
"love into the social direction. Thou in-
"fusest the generous principle, which makes
"him feel for sorrows not his own: nor
"feels he only, but, strange indeed! takes
"delight in rushing into foreign misery;
"and, with pleasure, goes to drop the pain-
"ful tear, over real or imaginary woes.
"Thy divine hand, thus strongly, drew the
"connecting tye, and linked man to man,
"by a sympathetic power; that nothing
"might be solitary or desolate in thy world;
"but all tend and work toward mutual as-
"sociation. For this great end, he is not
"left to a loose or arbitrary range of will.
"Thy wise decree hath erected within him
"a throne for virtue. There, thou hast
"not decked her with beauty only, to his
"admiring eye; but thrown around her,
"the awful effulgence of authority divine.
"Her persuasions have the force of a pre-
"cept; and her precepts are a law indispensible.

" sible. Man feels himself bound by this
" law, strict and immutable: and yet the pri-
" vilege of supererogating is left; a field o-
" pened for free and generous action; in
" which, performing a glorious course, he
" may attain the high reward, by thee al-
" lotted, of inward honour and self-esti-
" mation. Nothing is made superfluouf-
" ly severe, nothing left dangerously loose,
" in thy moral institution; but every active
" principle made to know its proper place.
" In just proportion, man's affection diver-
" ges from himself to objects around him.
" Where the diverging rays, too widely scat-
" tered, begin to lose their warmth; collect-
" ing them again by the idea of a public, a
" country, or the universe, thou rekindlest
" the dying flame. Converging eagerly to
" this point, behold how intense they glow!
" and man, tho' indifferent to each remote
" particular, burns with zeal for the whole.
" All things are by thee pre-ordained, great
" Mover of all! Throughout the wide ex-
" panse, every living creature runs a destin-
ed

" ed courſe. Whilſt all, under a law irre-
" ſiſtible, fulfil thy decrees, man alone ſeems
" to himſelf exempt; free to turn and bend
" his courſe at will. Yet is he not exempt:
" but, under the impreſſion of freedom, mi-
" niſters, in every action, to thy decree om-
" niponent, as much as the rolling ſun, or
" ebbing flood. What ſtrange contradic-
" tions are, in thy great ſcheme, reconciled!
" what glaring oppoſites made to agree!
" Neceſſity and liberty meet in the ſame a-
" gent, yet interfere not. He imagines
" himſelf free, yet is under the bonds of
" neceſſity. He diſcovers himſelf to be a
" neceſſary agent, and yet continues to act
" as he were free. Within the heart of
" man, thou haſt placed thy lamp, to direct
" his otherways uncertain ſteps. By this
" light, he is not only aſſured of the exiſ-
" tence, and entertained with all the glo-
" ries of the material world, but is enabl-
" ed to penetrate into the receſſes of nature.
" He perceives objects joined together by
" the myſterious link of cauſe and effect.
                                    " The

CONCLUSION.

"The connecting principle, tho' he can ne-
"ver explain, he is made to feel, and is
"thus instructed, how to refer even Things
"unknown, to their proper origin. Nay,
"he is taught by thee, to prophesy Things
"to come. Where reason is unavailing,
"instinct comes in aid, and bestows a pow-
"er of divination, which discovers the fu-
"ture, by the past. Thus, thou gradually
"liftest him up to the knowledge of thy-
"self. The plain and simple sense, which,
"in the most obvious effect, reads and per-
"ceives a cause, brings him streight to thee,
"the first great cause, the antient of days,
"the eternal source of all. Thou present-
"est thyself to us, and we cannot avoid thee.
"We must doubt of our own existence, if
"we call in question thine. We see thee
"by thine own light. We see thee, not
"existing only, but in wisdom and in bene-
"volence supreme, as in existence, first. As
"spots in the sun's bright orb, so in the u-
"niversal plan, scattered evils are lost in the
"blaze of superabundant goodness. Even,
"by

"by the research of human reason, weak as it is, those seeming evils diminish and fly away apace. Objects, supposed superfluous or noxious, have assumed a beneficial aspect. How much more, to thine all penetrating eye, must all appear excellent and fair! It must be so. We cannot doubt. Neither imperfection nor malice dwell with thee. Thou appointest as salutary, what we lament as painful. What mortals term sin, thou pronouncest to be only error. For moral evil vanishes, in some measure, from before thy more perfect sight: and as, at the beginning of days, thou saw'st, so thou seest, and pronouncest still, that *every thing thou hast made is good.*"

Titles in This Series

1: Beattie, James. AN ESSAY ON THE NATURE AND IMMUTABILITY OF TRUTH. 1770.

2: Brown, Thomas. OBSERVATIONS ON THE NATURE AND TENDENCY OF THE DOCTRINE OF MR. HUME, CONCERNING THE RELATION OF CAUSE AND EFFECT. 2nd ed. 1806.

3: Burton, John Hill. LIFE AND CORRESPONDENCE OF DAVID HUME. 1846.

4: Campbell, George. A DISSERTATION ON MIRACLES. 1762.

5: Graham, Henry Grey. SCOTTISH MEN OF LETTERS IN THE EIGHTEENTH CENTURY. 1908.

6: Greig, J.Y.T. DAVID HUME. 1931.

7: Hendel, Charles W. STUDIES IN THE PHILOSOPHY OF DAVID HUME. 2nd ed. 1963.

8: Home, Henry, Lord Kames. ESSAYS ON THE PRIN-

CIPLES OF MORALITY AND NATURAL RELIGION. 1751.

9: Hume, David. THE LETTERS OF DAVID HUME. Edited by J.Y.T. Greig. 1932.

10: Hume, David. NEW LETTERS OF DAVID HUME. Edited by Raymond Klibansky and Ernest C. Mossner. 1954.

11: Jacobi, Friedrich Heinrich. DAVID HUME ÜBER DEN GLAUBEN, ODER IDEALISMUS UND REALISMUS. Ein Gespräch. 1787.
with
———. VORREDE, ZUGLEICH EINLEITUNG IN DES VERFASSERS SÄMMTLICHE PHILOSOPHISCHE SCHRIFTEN. 1815.

12: Jessop, T. E. A BIBLIOGRAPHY OF DAVID HUME AND OF SCOTTISH PHILOSOPHY FROM FRANCES HUTCHESON TO LORD BALFOUR. 1938.

13: Kemp Smith, Norman. THE PHILOSOPHY OF DAVID HUME. 1941.

14: Kuypers, Mary Shaw. STUDIES IN THE EIGHTEENTH CENTURY BACKGROUND OF HUME'S EMPIRICISM. 1930.

15: Laird, John. HUME'S PHILOSOPHY OF HUMAN NATURE. 1932.

16: Priestley, Joseph. LETTERS TO A PHILOSOPHICAL UNBELIEVER. Part I. 1817.

17: Salmon, C. V. THE CENTRAL PROBLEM OF DAVID HUME'S PHILOSOPHY. 1929.

18: Seth, Andrew. SCOTTISH PHILOSOPHY. 1890.